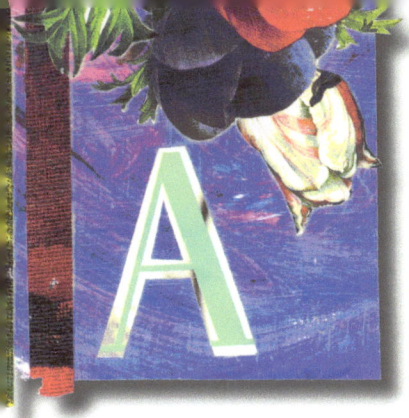

AN ALPHABET BOOK OF THOUGHTS TO
PERHAPS PERCEIVE LIFE IN A NEW WAY,
FEATURING ART,
PHOTOGRAPHY
AND COLLAGE

*My hands make the voice
of my heart visible.*
— Maarten Schaddelee

JUST PASSING THROUGH

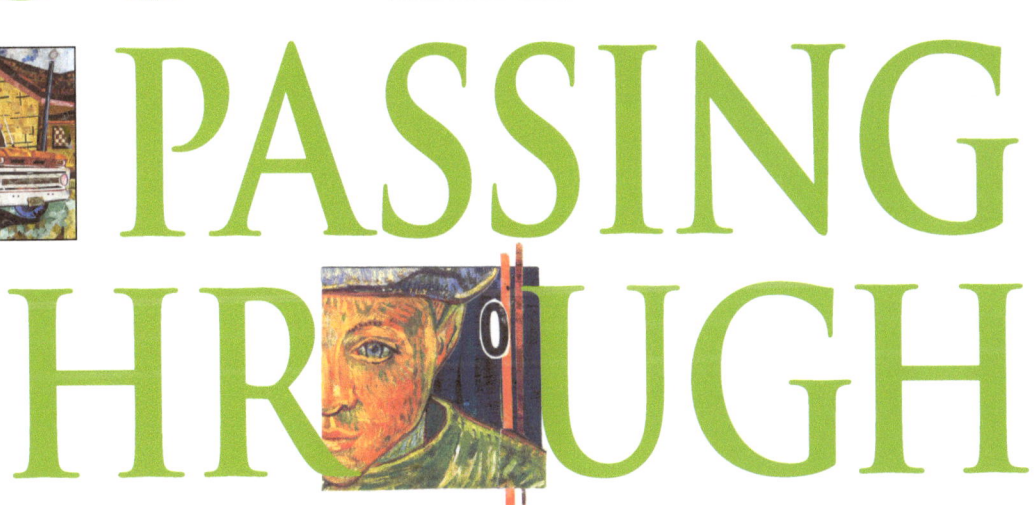

DAN & MARSHA BATCHELOR

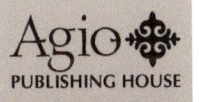

Agio
PUBLISHING HOUSE

151 Howe Street, Victoria BC Canada V8V 4K5

For information and bulk orders, please contact
info@agiopublishing.com *or go to*
www.agiopublishing.com

ISBN 978-1-897435-38-0 (paperback)

10 9 8 7 6 5 4 3 2 1

Printed on acid-free paper made without fibre from endangered old-growth forests.

Copyright © 2010, Dan Batchelor and Marsha Batchelor. All rights reserved.

Photography by DanBatchelor.com
Artwork, collages and layout by Marsha Batchelor.
Commentary written by Marsha and Dan Batchelor.
Quotations are believed to be in the public domain.

No part of this publication may be reproduced, stored in or introduced into a retrieval system, or transmitted, in any form or by any means (electronic, mechanical, photocopying, recording or otherwise), without the prior written permission of both copyright owners and the publisher of this book.

Collages contain small portions of larger artwork pieces for which a copyright may be held by the artist, their estate and/or Bigstockphoto, istockphoto or Shutterstock.

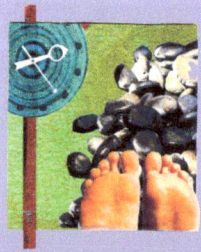

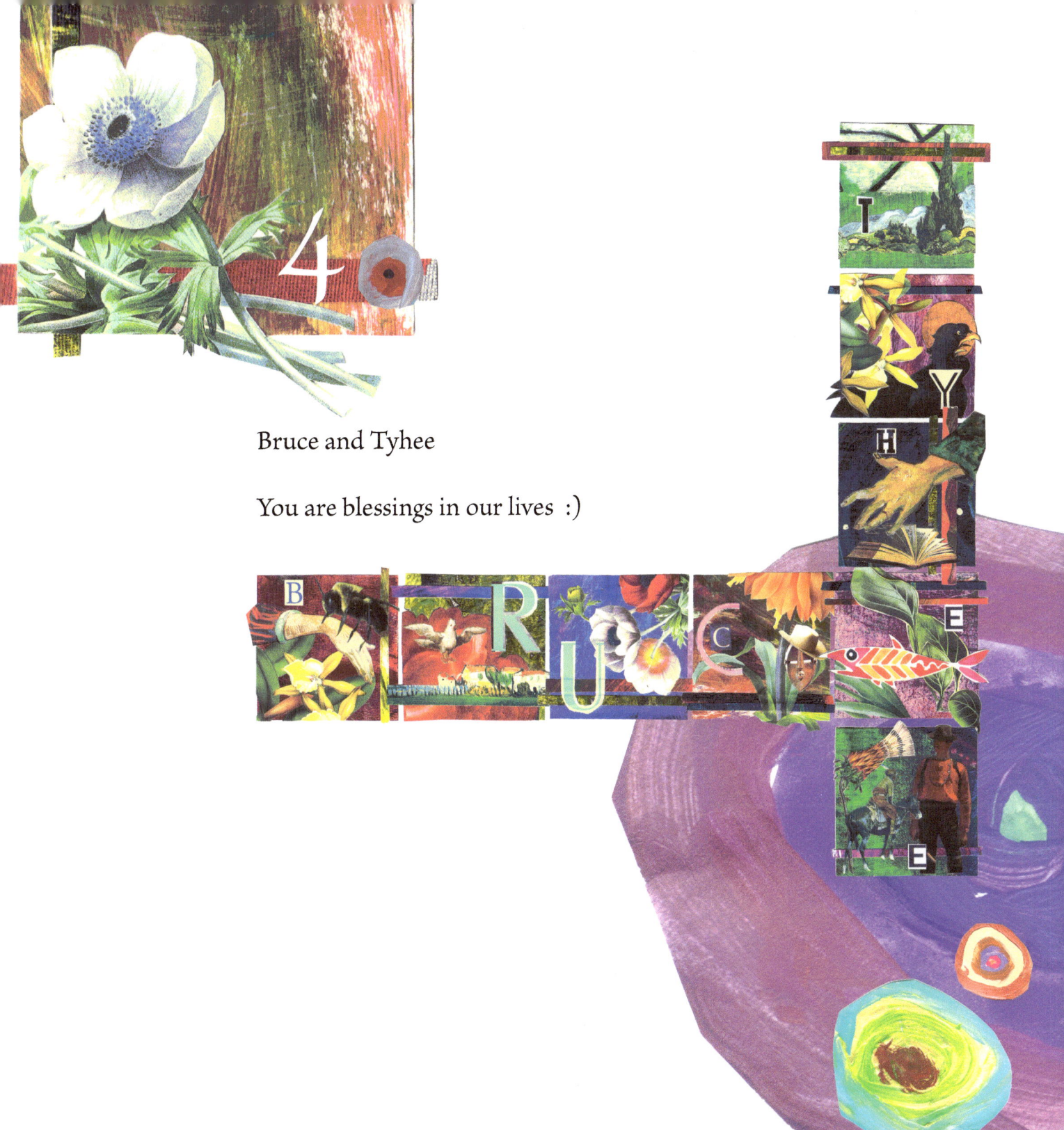

Bruce and Tyhee

You are blessings in our lives :)

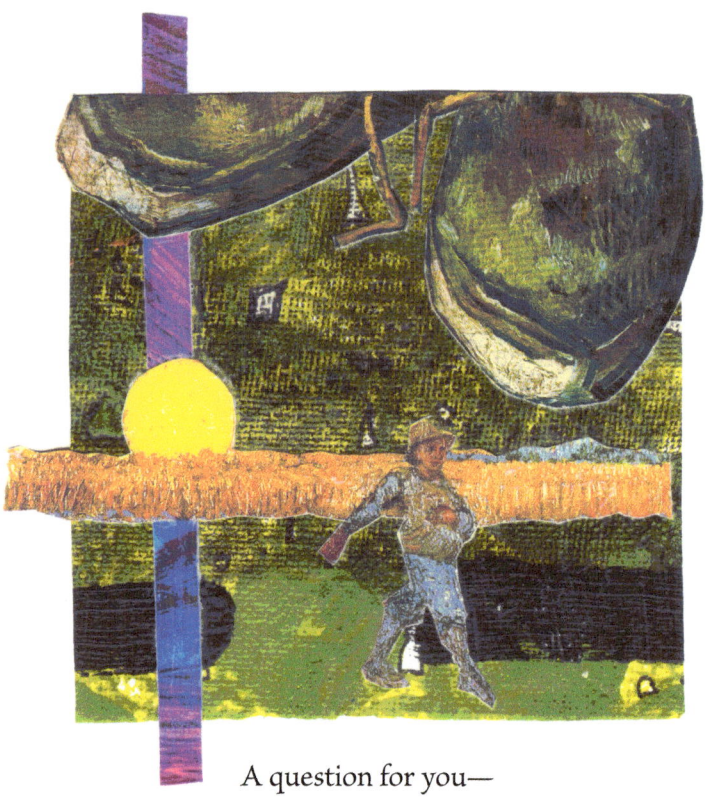

A question for you—

Does our environment create us, or do we create our environment?

Hi

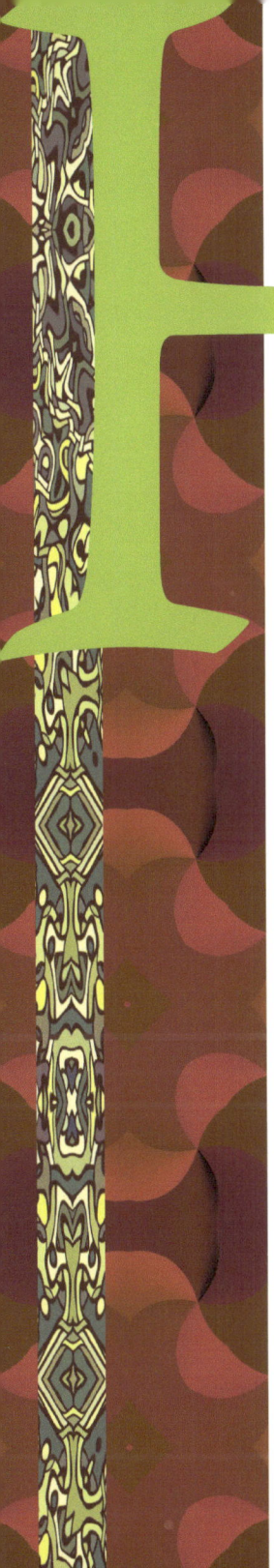

Thanks for choosing to pick up this book to have a look. It is a cathartic piece of work that we have created for two reasons.

First, I, Marsha, have had many thoughts over the years regarding how to understand the ever-spinning wheel of life that goes round and round, often coming back to where I was before, as I try to catch my breath to be able to see the cause and effects of my choices and actions. Dan has grown up with this inquiring perspective and we thought that maybe our combined ideas could help others with their own journeys. These 26 thoughts help to slow down the spin and remind us that our everyday thoughts are extremely important. It's like a jigsaw puzzle—finding a piece that fits, YAHOO—now look for another!

Second, we are both artists always looking for ways to display our work. What better way than to create a book together! As we are all *just passing through* in this life, we are offered abundant opportunities and can accomplish anything that we set our minds on! Again and again and again.

The world's our oyster. Life's a bowl of cherries. Not sure if you want to eat them together though… :)

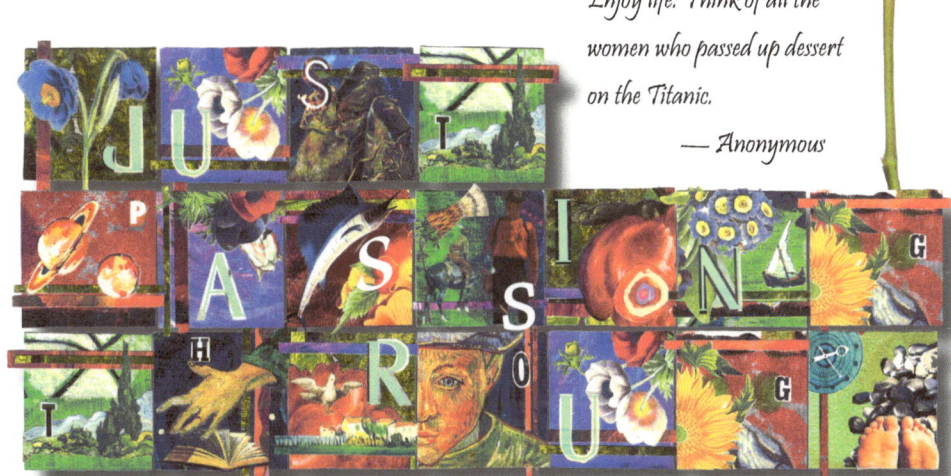

Enjoy life. Think of all the women who passed up dessert on the Titanic.
— Anonymous

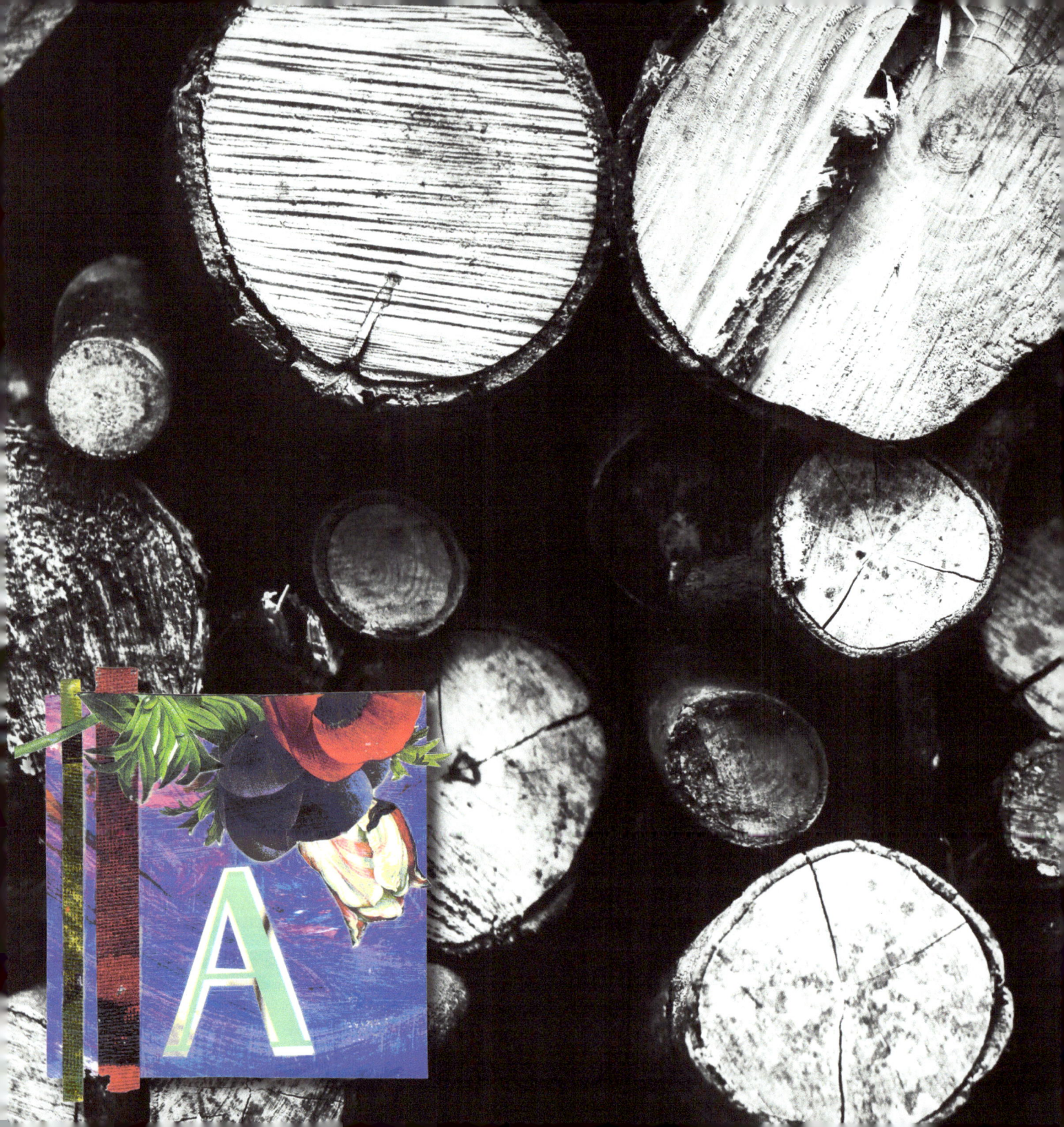

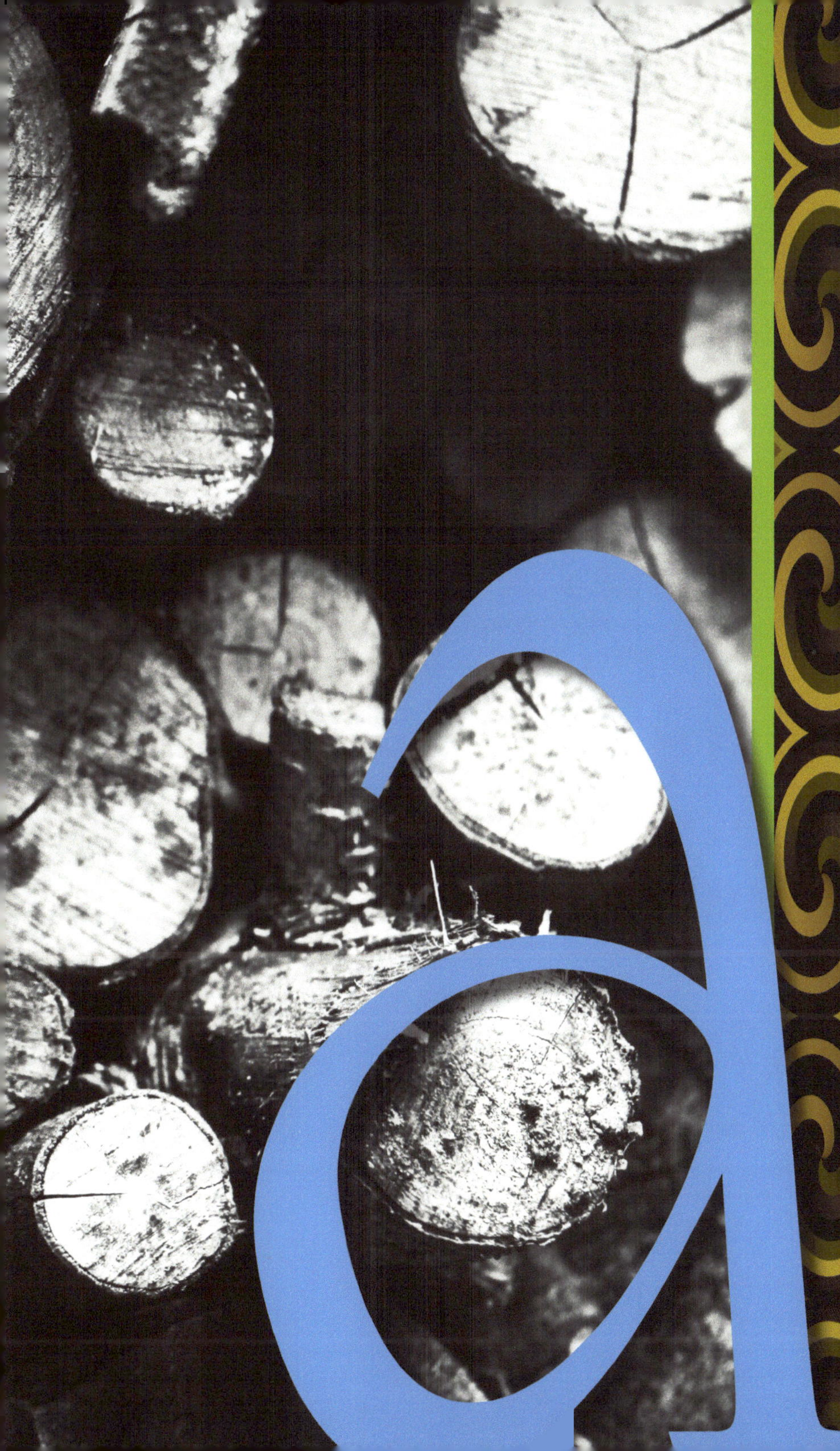

All by yourself, you can create a loving world. By changing your own behaviour and thoughts in small ways, you offer others around you, by example, new options of thought and choice. Live your life purposefully. Choose your own direction instead of walking in others' footsteps.

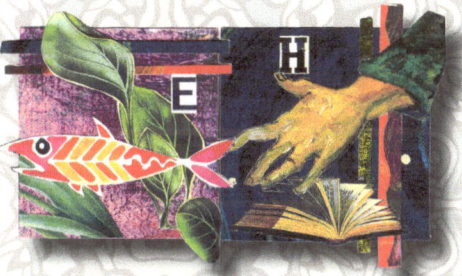

Men acquire a particular quality by constantly acting a particular way. We become just by performing just actions, temperate by performing temperate actions, brave by performing brave actions.
— Aristotle

Clean your finger before you point at my spots.
— Benjamin Franklin

B

BARAKA BASHAD

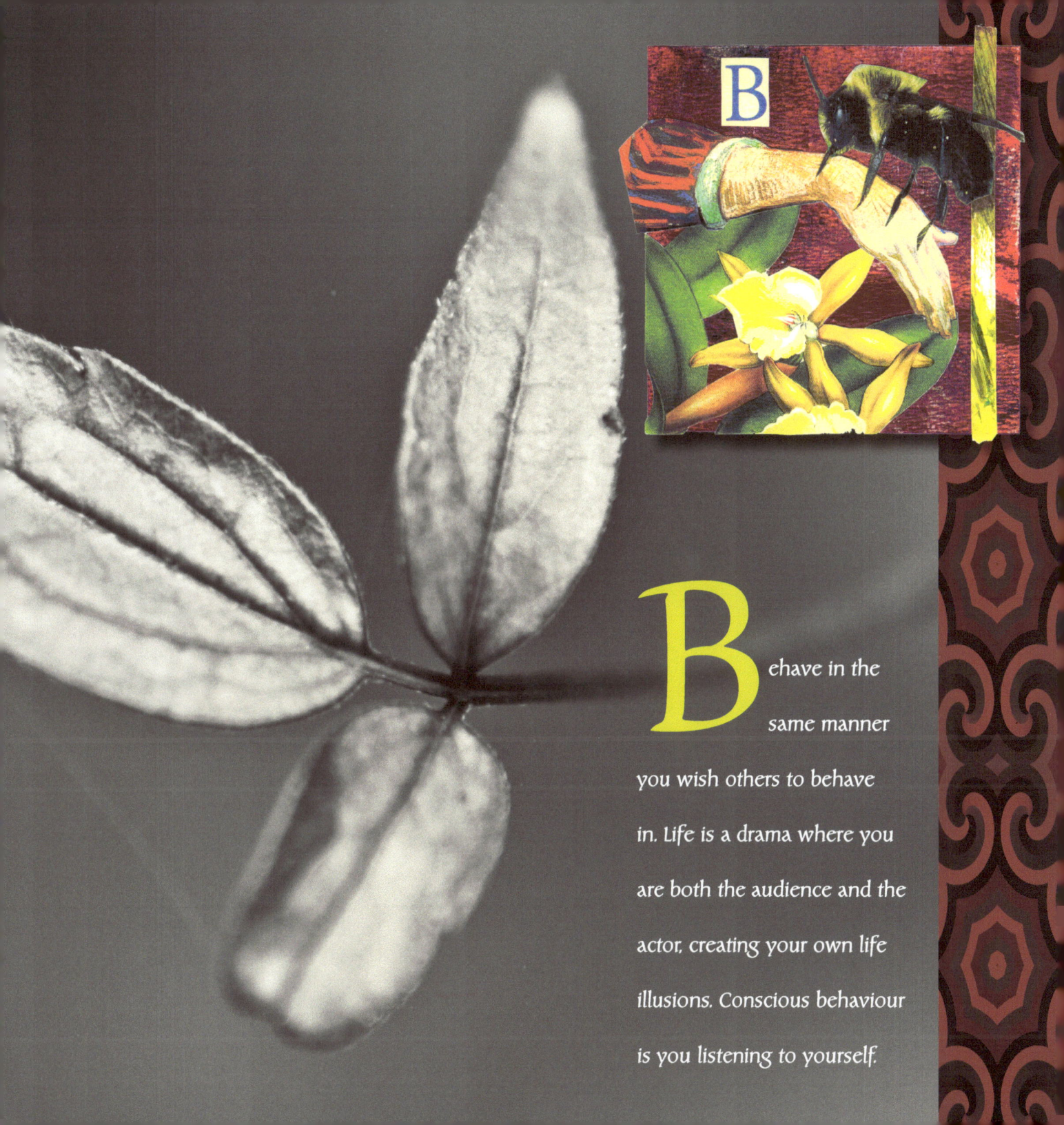

Behave in the same manner you wish others to behave in. Life is a drama where you are both the audience and the actor, creating your own life illusions. Conscious behaviour is you listening to yourself.

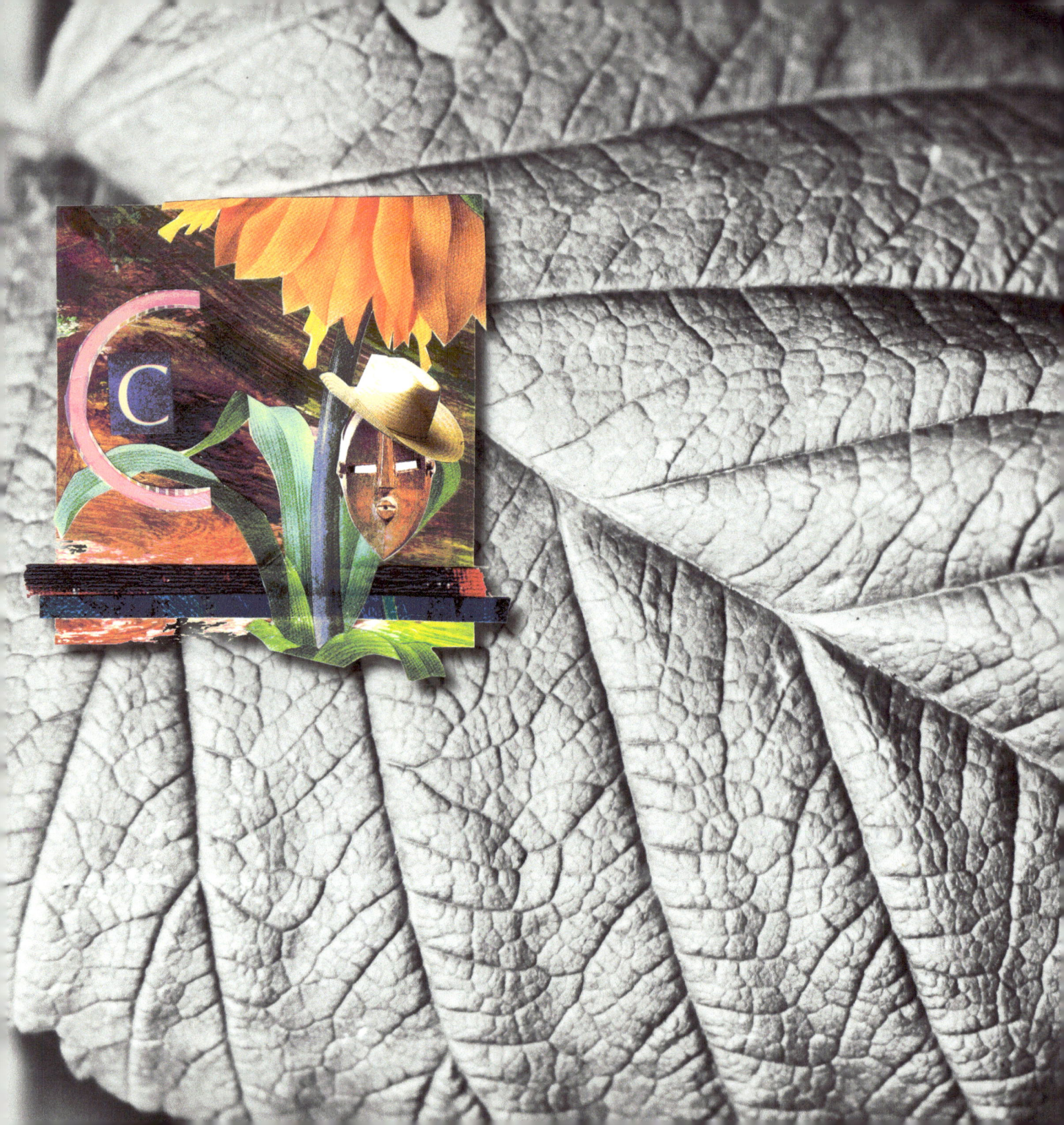

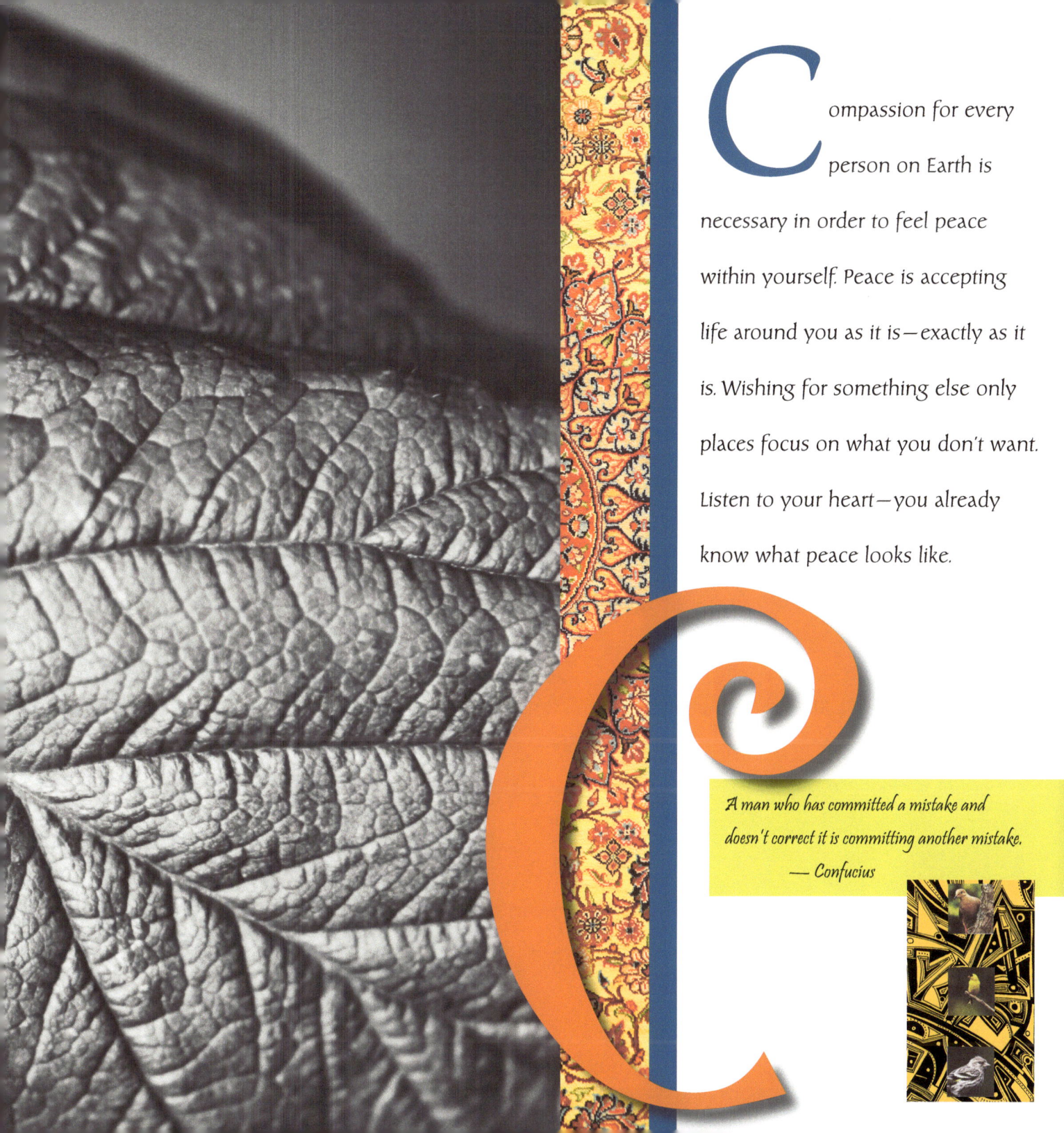

Compassion for every person on Earth is necessary in order to feel peace within yourself. Peace is accepting life around you as it is—exactly as it is. Wishing for something else only places focus on what you don't want. Listen to your heart—you already know what peace looks like.

A man who has committed a mistake and doesn't correct it is committing another mistake.
— *Confucius*

Death of our real selves is a creative illusion on Earth. All the people we know and the material things we have are part of the passing show— even our physical bodies— they are all temporary and have been lent to us to create our own illusions. Physical dying is just a doorway, because all Souls will continue to learn, live and love forever.

You will find, as you look back upon your life, that the moments when you really lived are the moments when you have done things in the spirit of love.
— Henry Drummond

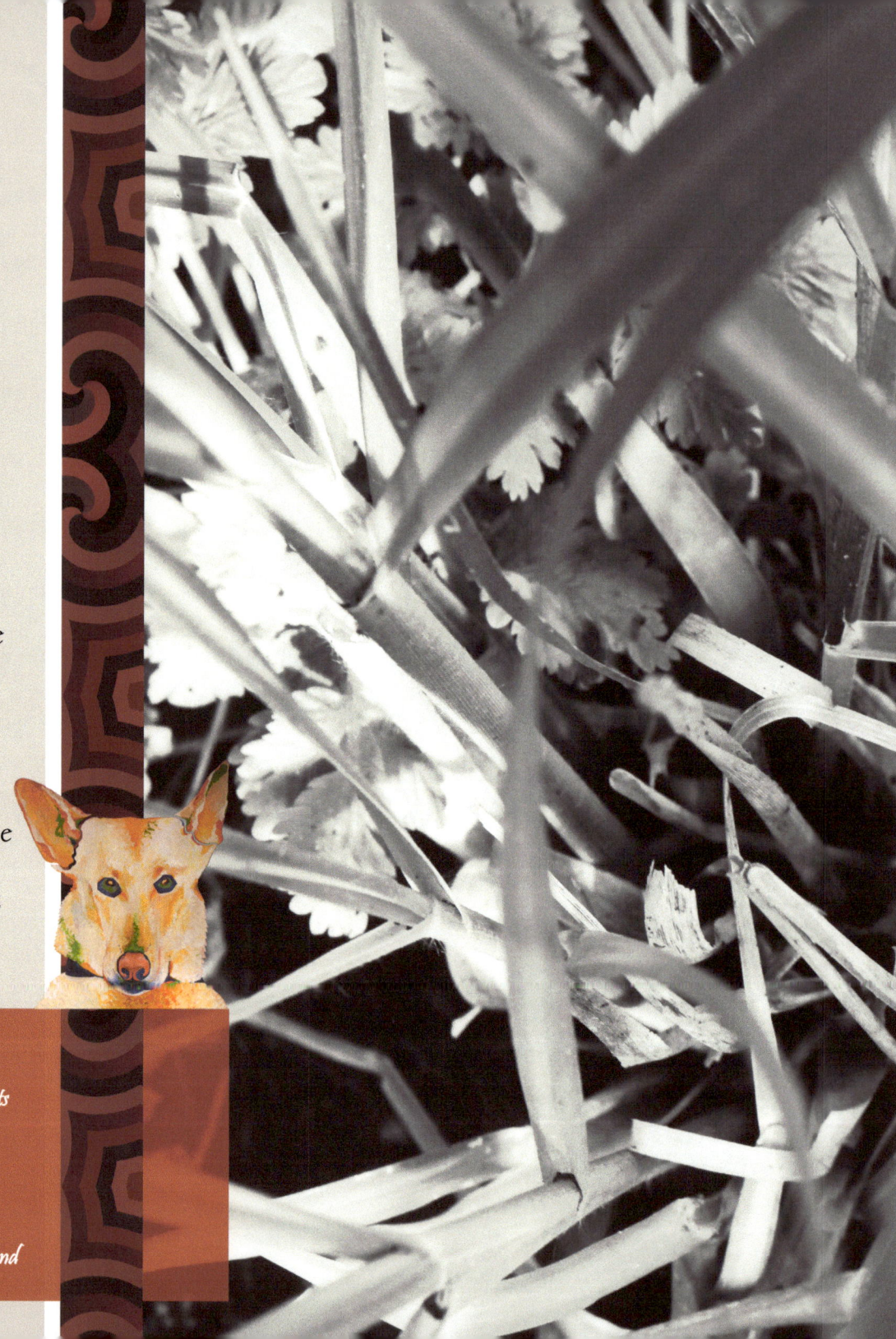

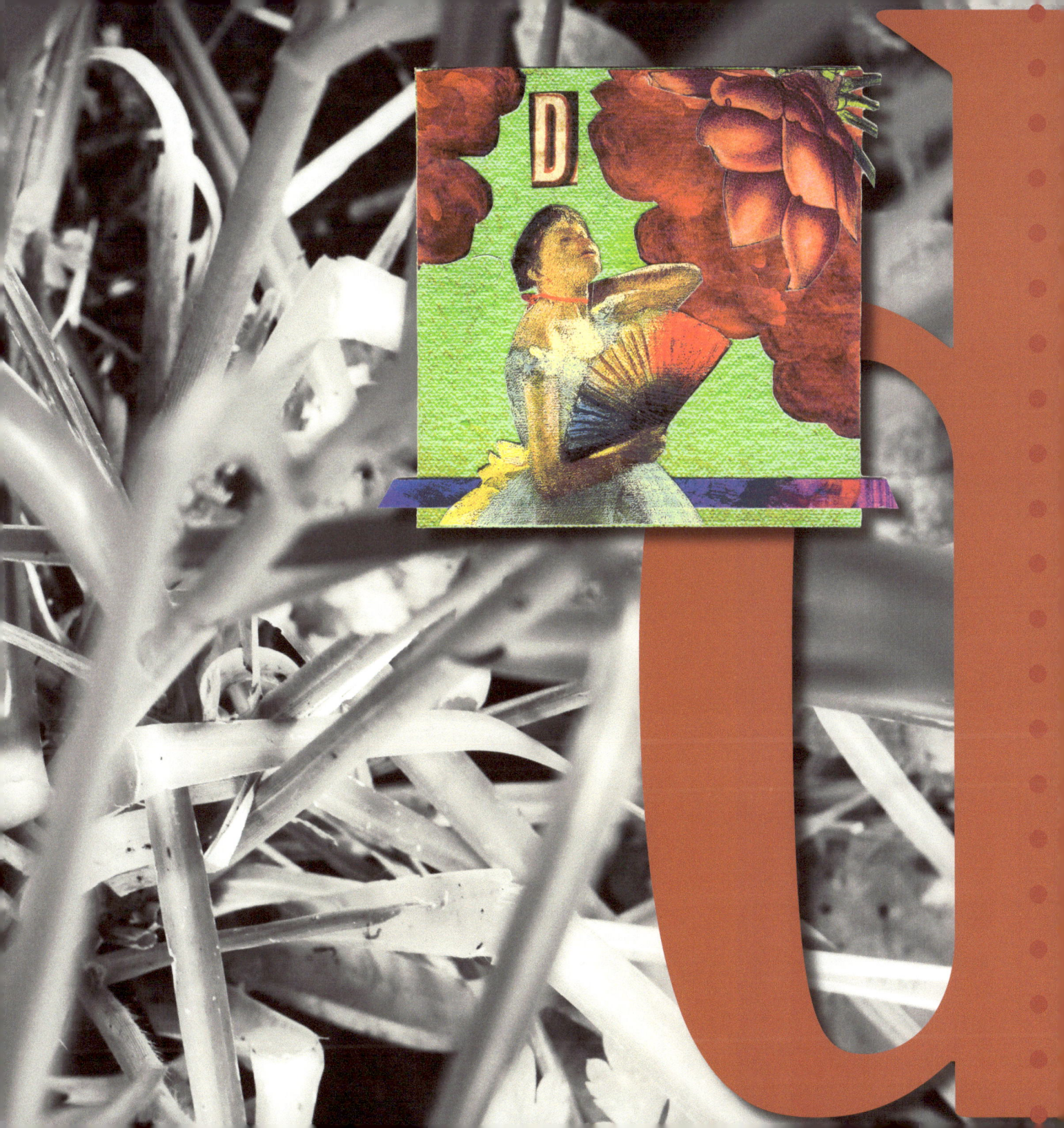

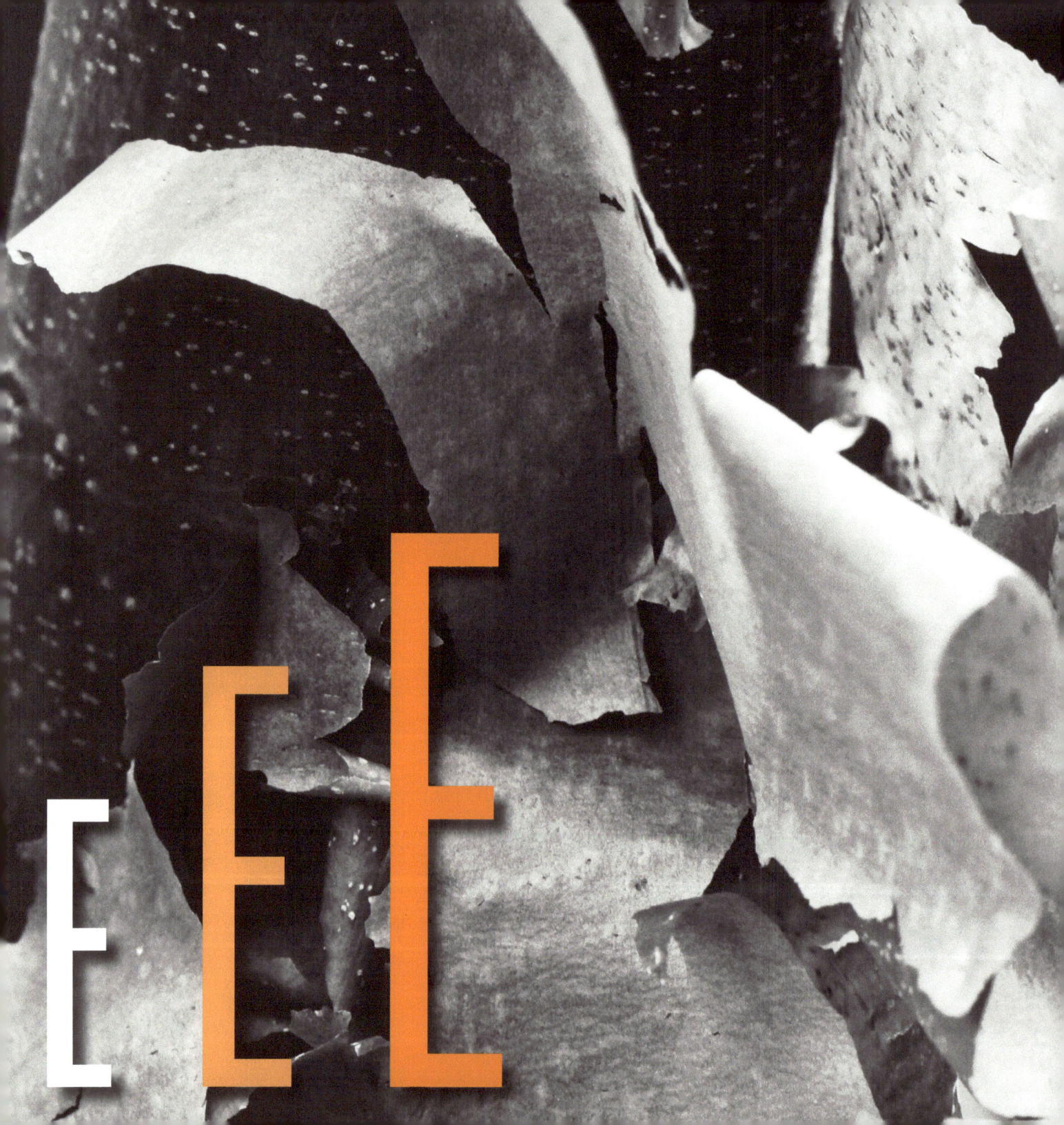

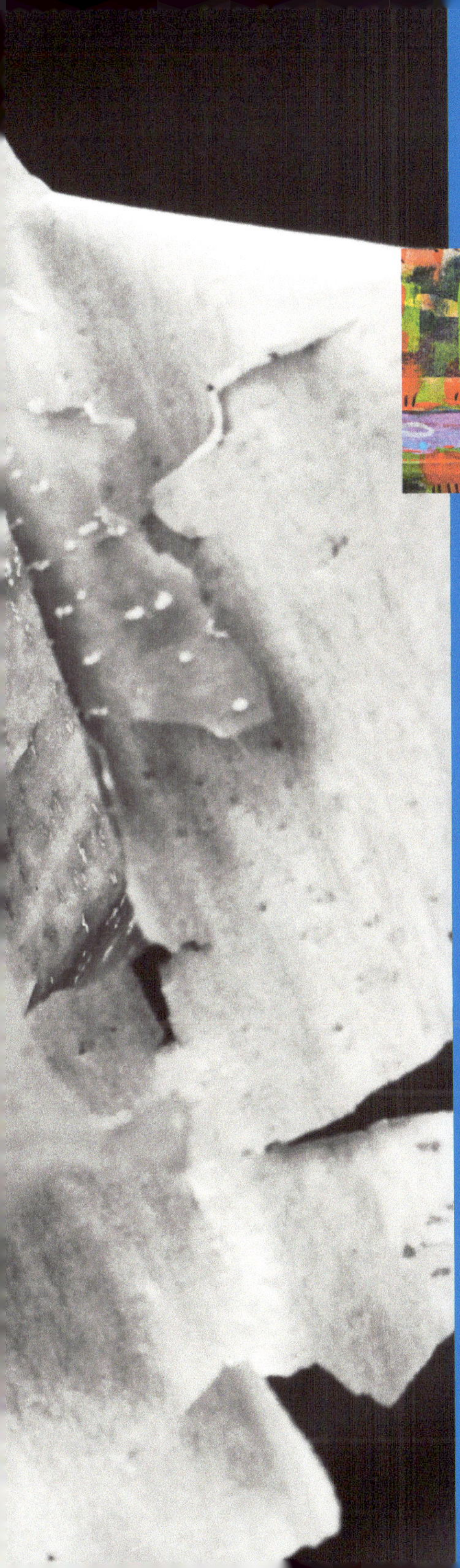

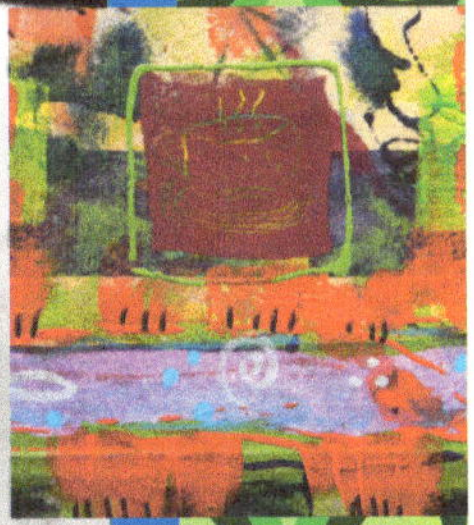

Experiences in your life are not good or bad, they are simply blessings and opportunities to learn and grow spiritually. When something seems bad, ask from your heart, "What can I learn from this situation?" Listen to your inner voice and you will get an answer to find personal growth. Gratitude for this opportunity is needed in order to see clearly.

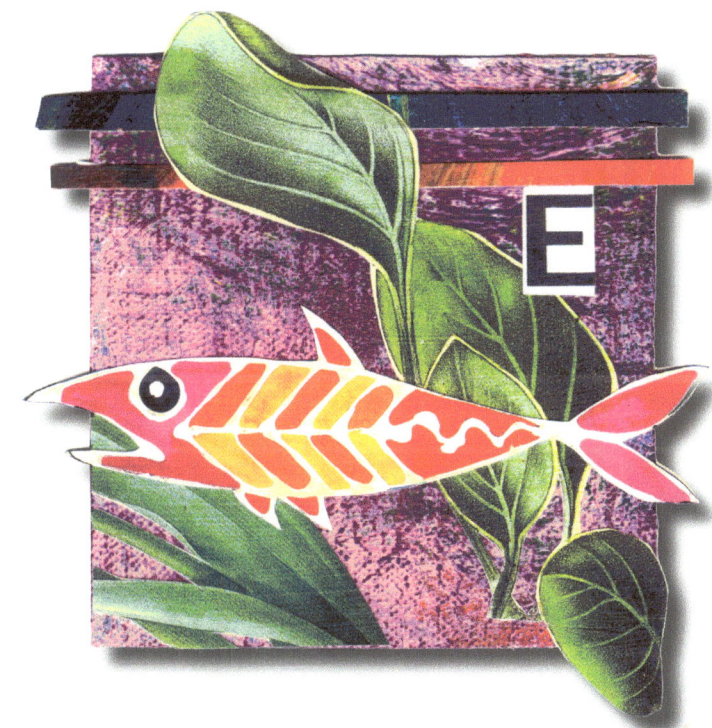

When the blessings of Spirit are given to us without struggle, we don't recognize the treasure that is in our hands.
— Eckankar Spiritual Leader Harold Klemp

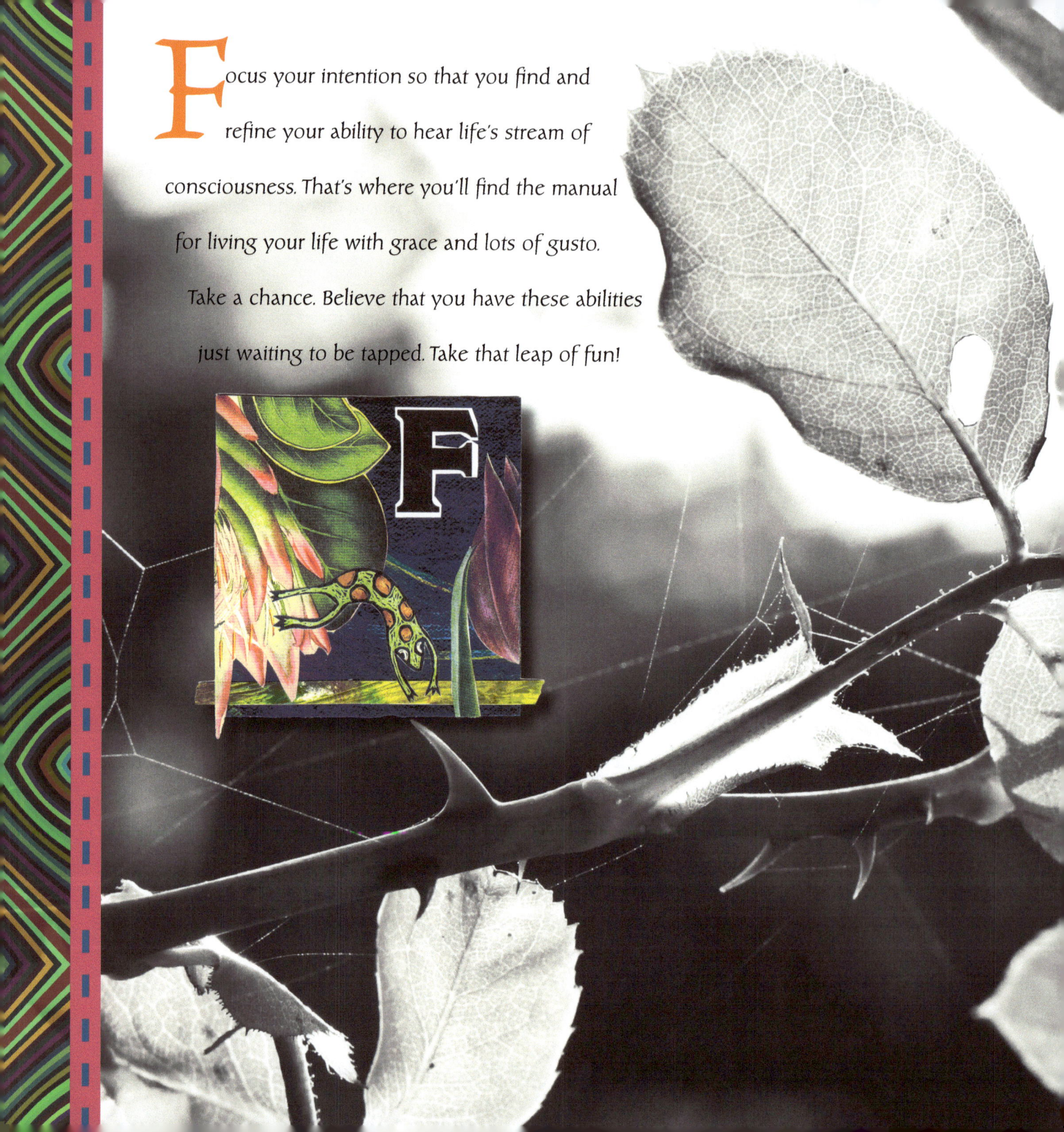

Focus your intention so that you find and refine your ability to hear life's stream of consciousness. That's where you'll find the manual for living your life with grace and lots of gusto. Take a chance. Believe that you have these abilities just waiting to be tapped. Take that leap of fun!

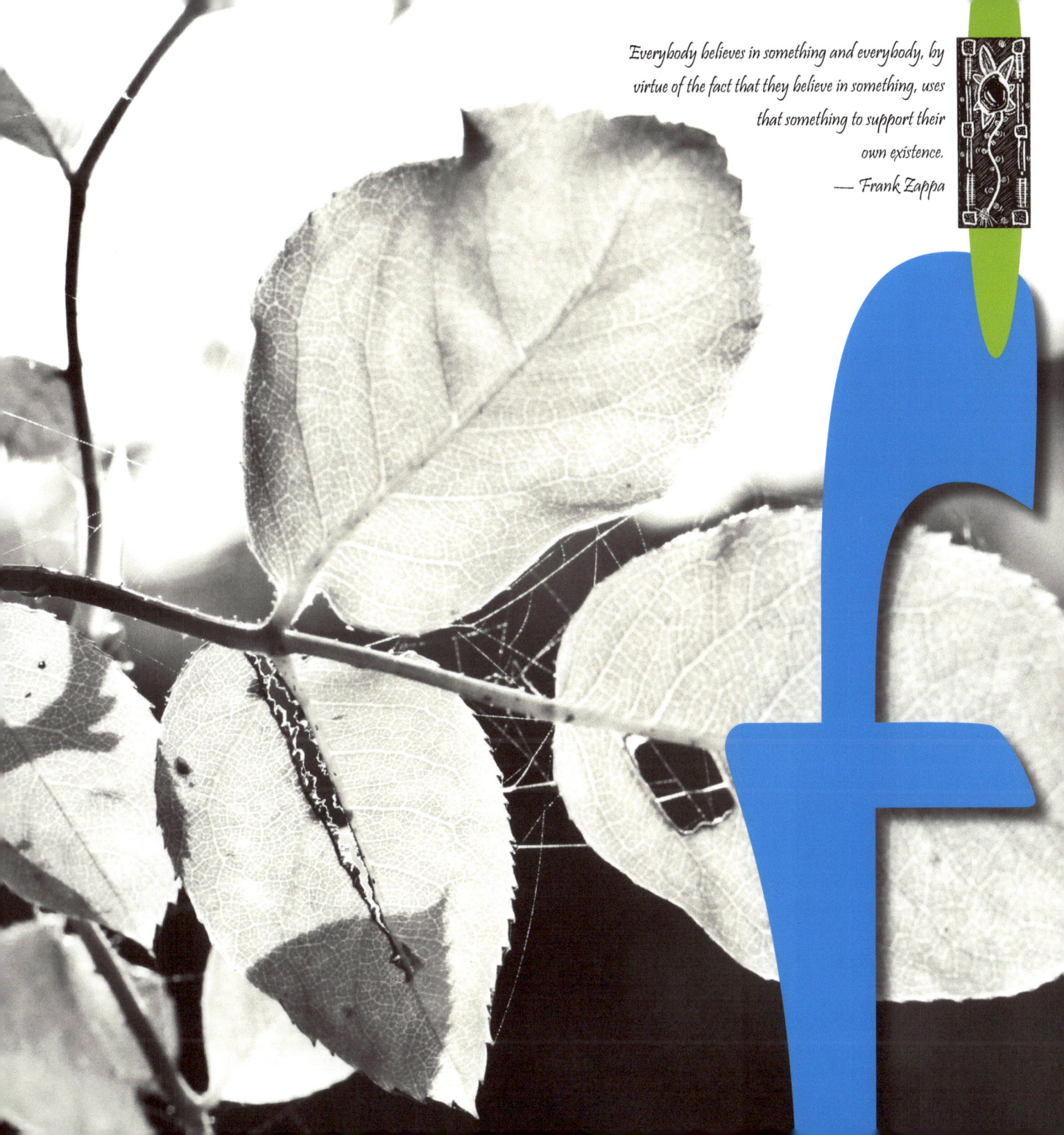

Everybody believes in something and everybody, by virtue of the fact that they believe in something, uses that something to support their own existence.

— Frank Zappa

Gently with gratitude, believe in ourselves and others as we seek, learn, and take our next step in life. Everything around us is in perfect purposeful harmony—it is up to us to choose to see it that way. Think harmony as we teach ourselves in this lifetime through our choices and mistakes. After all, isn't that what we are here to do—learn to love?

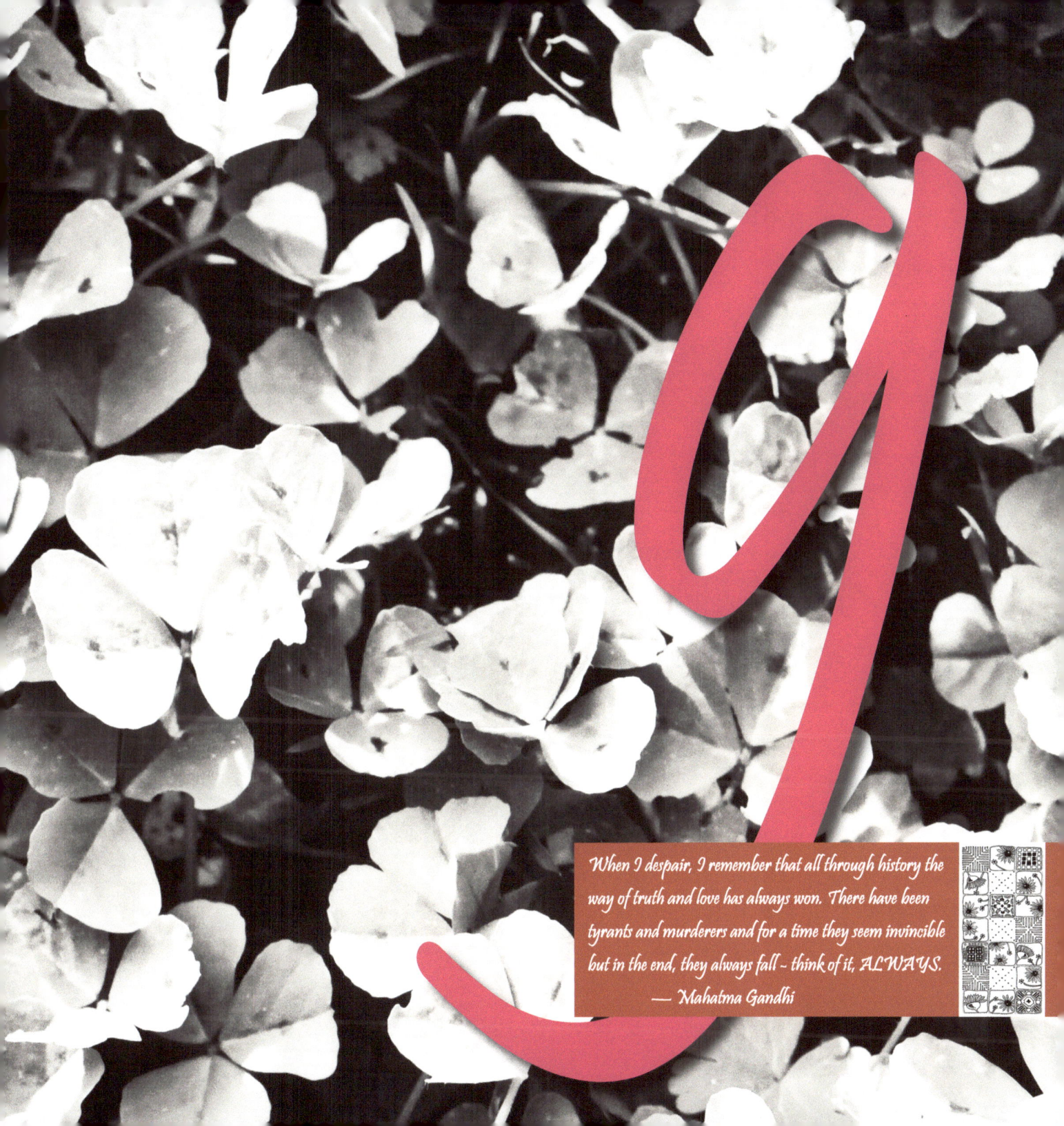

When I despair, I remember that all through history the way of truth and love has always won. There have been tyrants and murderers and for a time they seem invincible but in the end, they always fall - think of it, ALWAYS.
— Mahatma Gandhi

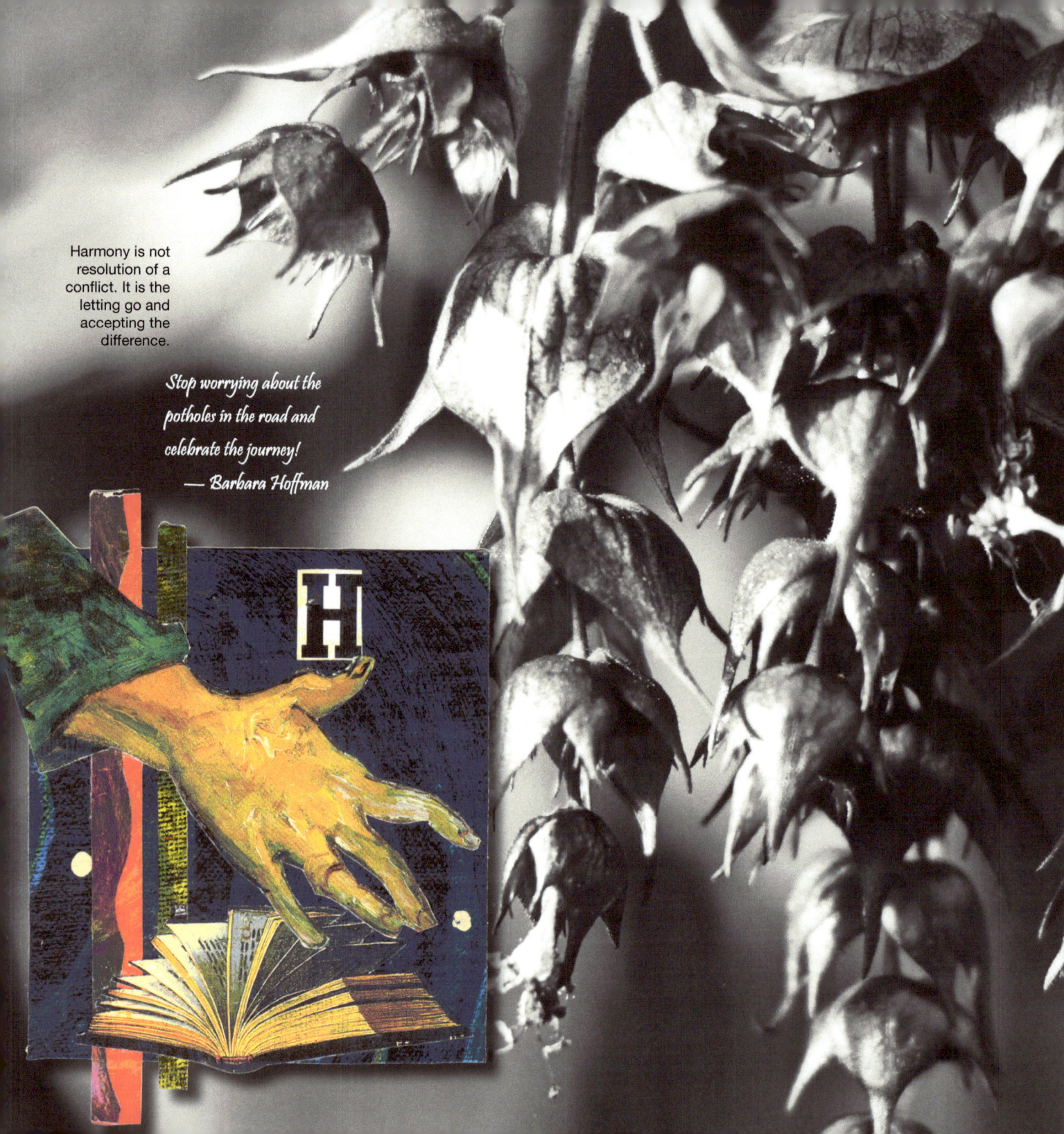

Harmony is not resolution of a conflict. It is the letting go and accepting the difference.

Stop worrying about the potholes in the road and celebrate the journey!
— *Barbara Hoffman*

Humour is a choice and reflection of a divine love. We can, and must learn to, choose to see life as light-hearted no matter what the circumstance. Laughing at turmoil, laughing with others and at ourselves heals our physical and mental bodies by supporting our spiritual selves. lol !

HUUU

Intention is the choosing of a reality that you wish to manifest. Every thought we have (the cause) has an effect that will be played out in the future. Be it desired or not. Choose your daily thoughts carefully because that is how you are creating your life. If you don't like your life — change your thoughts.

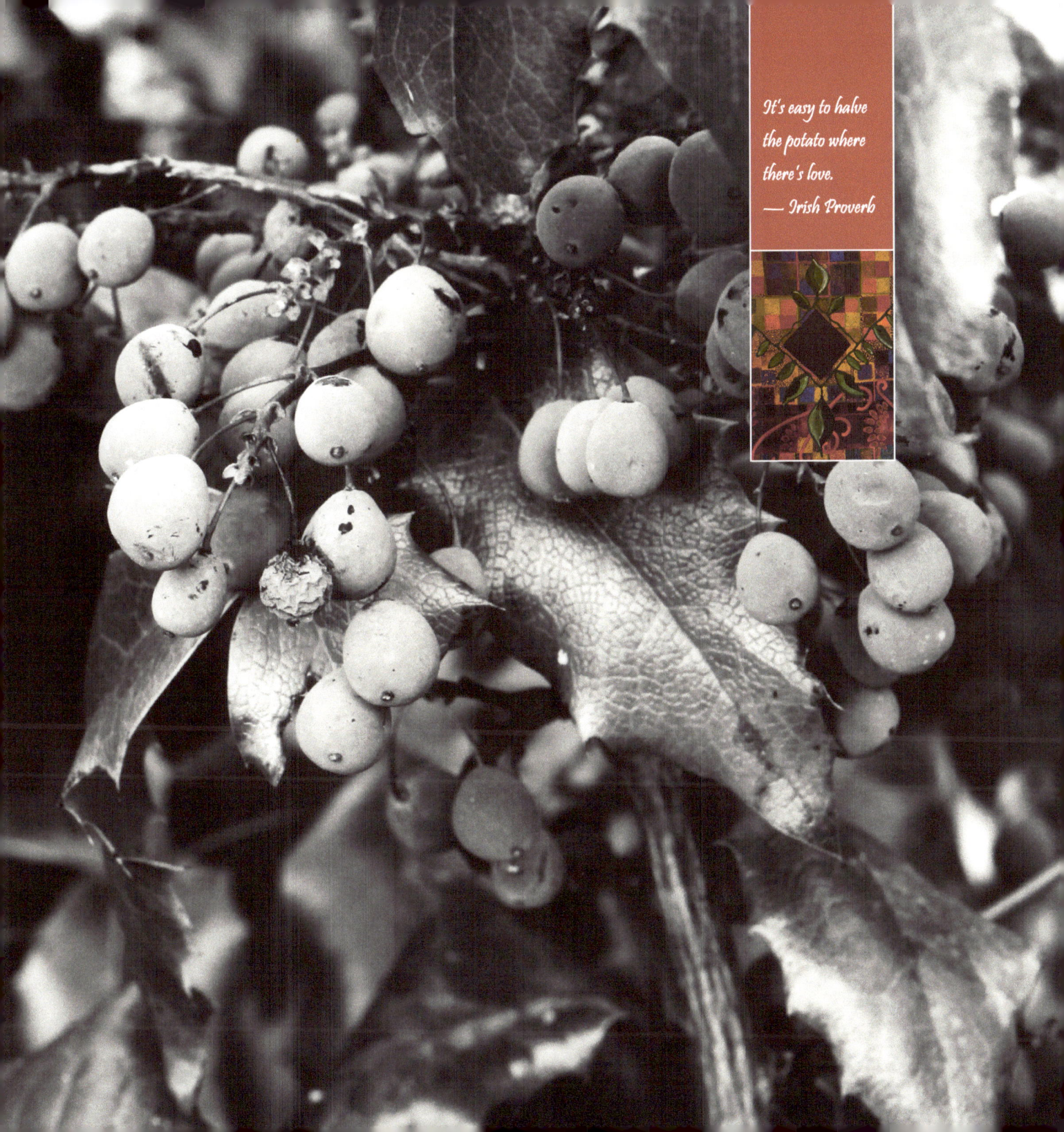

It's easy to halve the potato where there's love.
— *Irish Proverb*

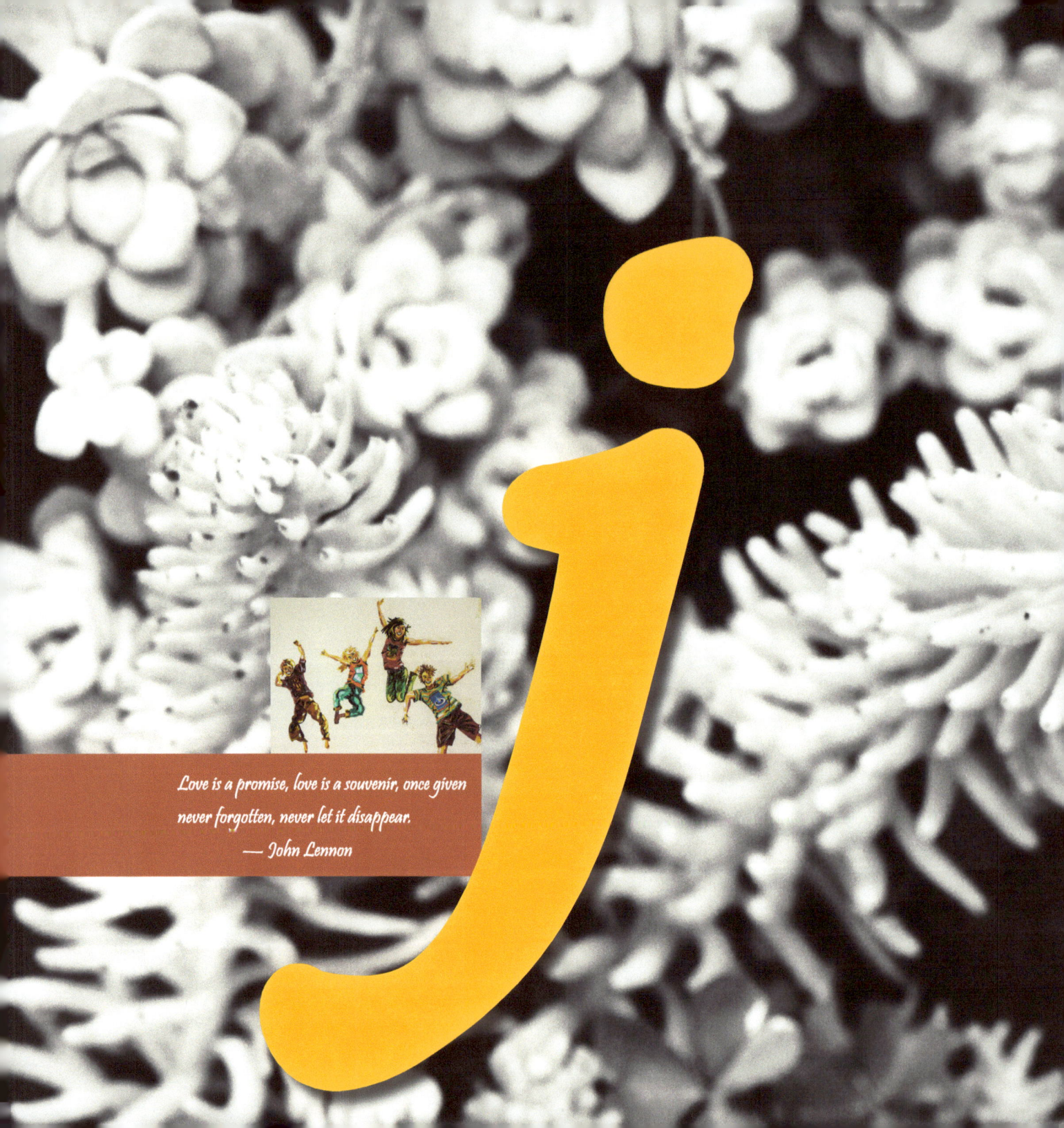

Love is a promise, love is a souvenir, once given never forgotten, never let it disappear.
— John Lennon

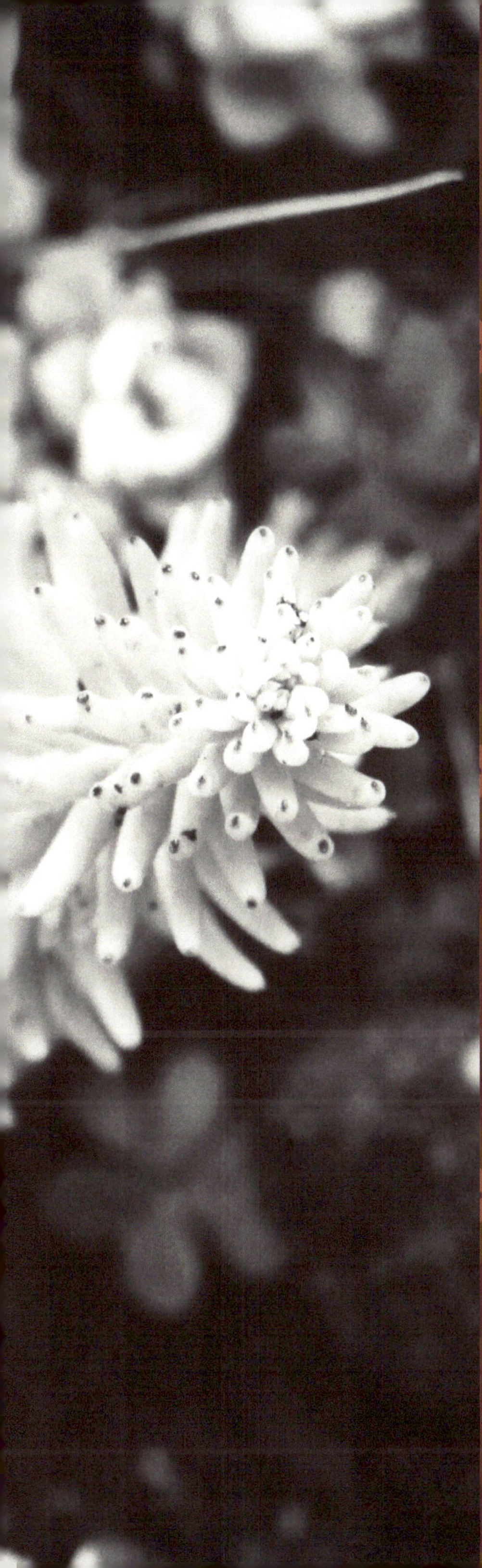

Judging other peoples thoughts, actions and choices creates a karma that will need to be balanced in the future. Think of everyone, including yourself, as a spark of Divine Source and step away from judgement. Treat everyone you meet with respect and give them space to be who they are. Only look inside yourself while always being humble.

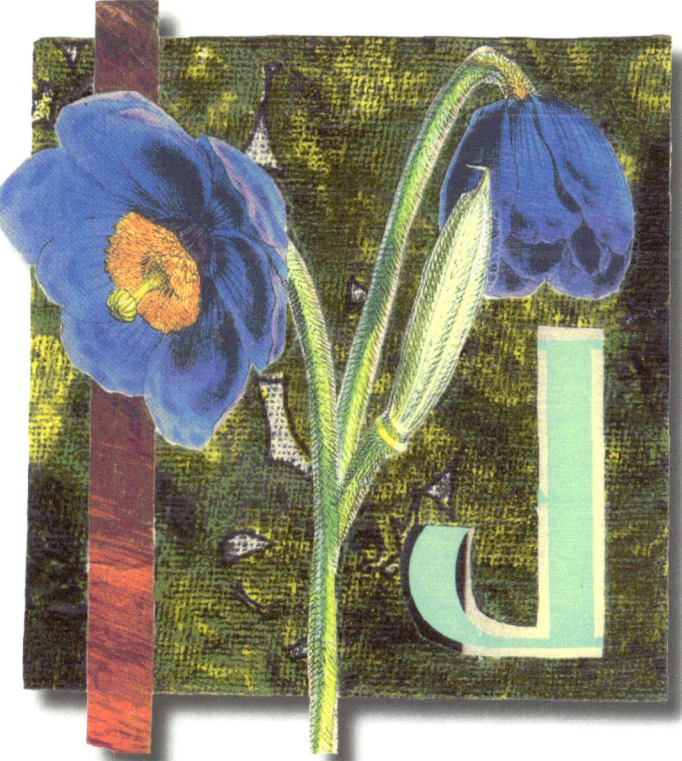

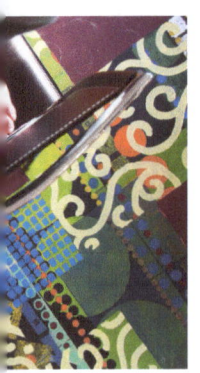

If you make a meal, put love into it instead of the frustrations of your day. Because whatever is put into the food is a reflection of what you have inside yourself, and it goes out to your family, it goes out to your friends. And it makes a very real difference.
— *Harold Klemp*

Knowing ourselves...

Our job is to get to know ourselves. Not someone else. When we are able to treat everyone equally with caring and compassion then we will really and truly know who we are inside and out.

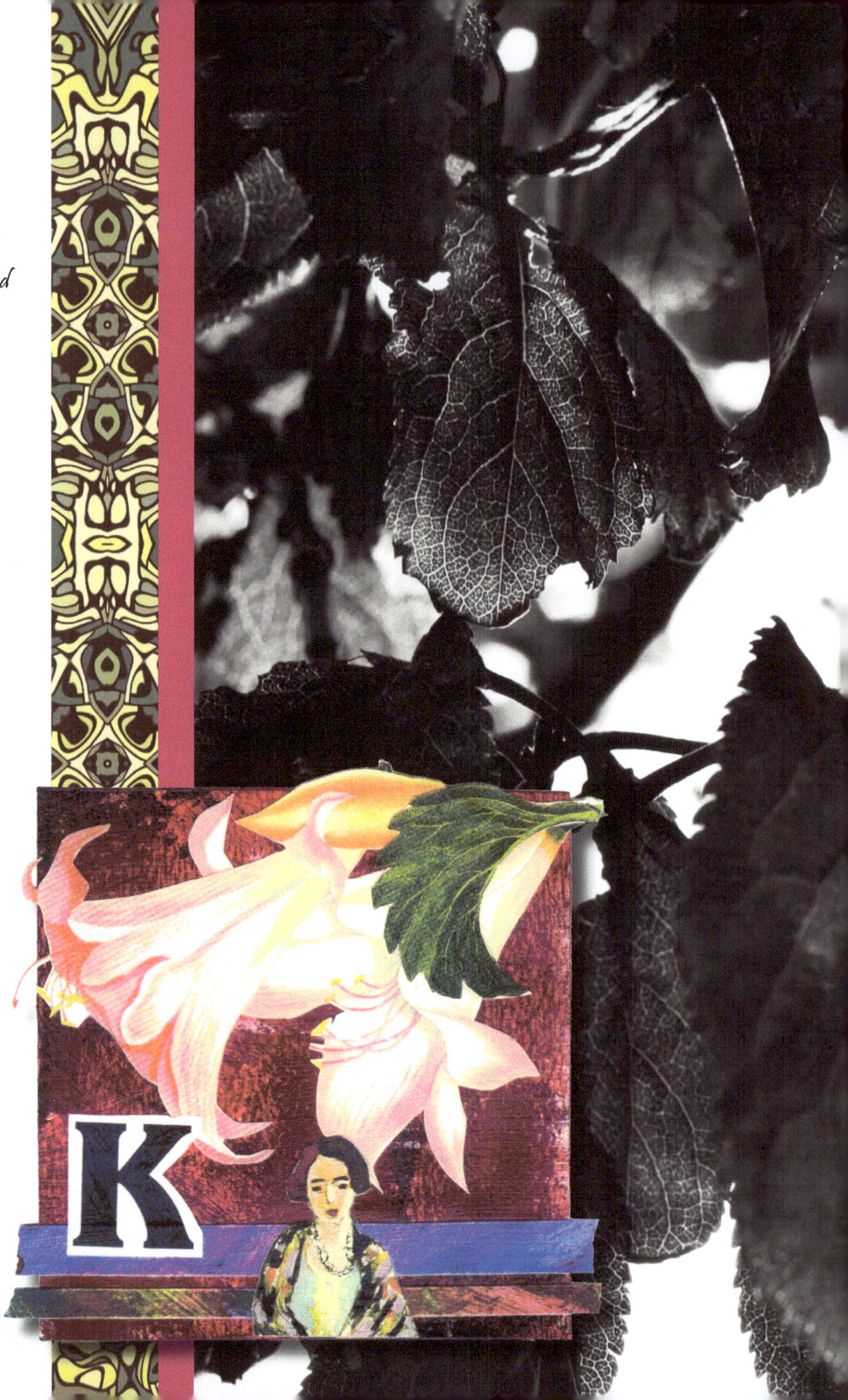

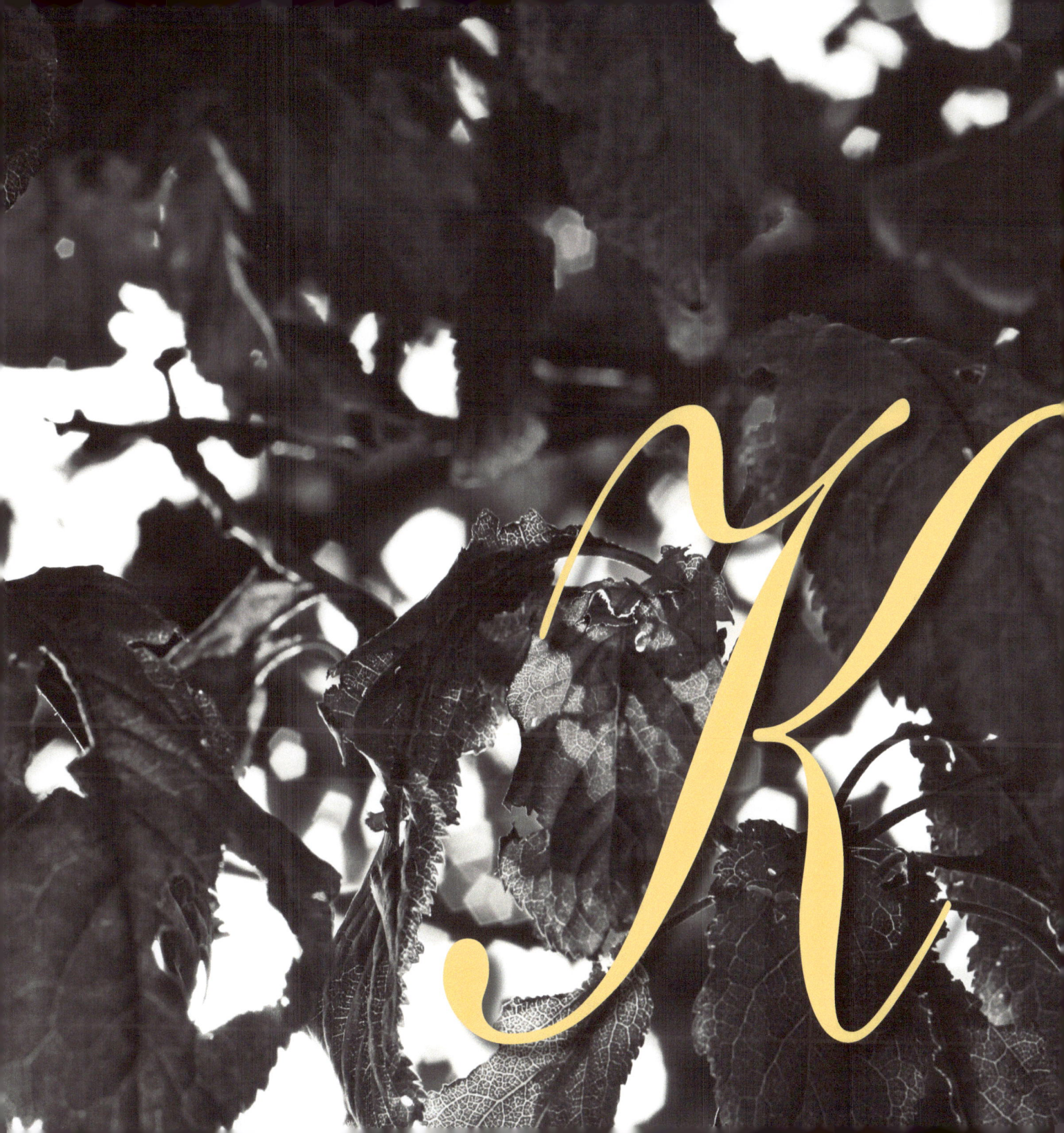

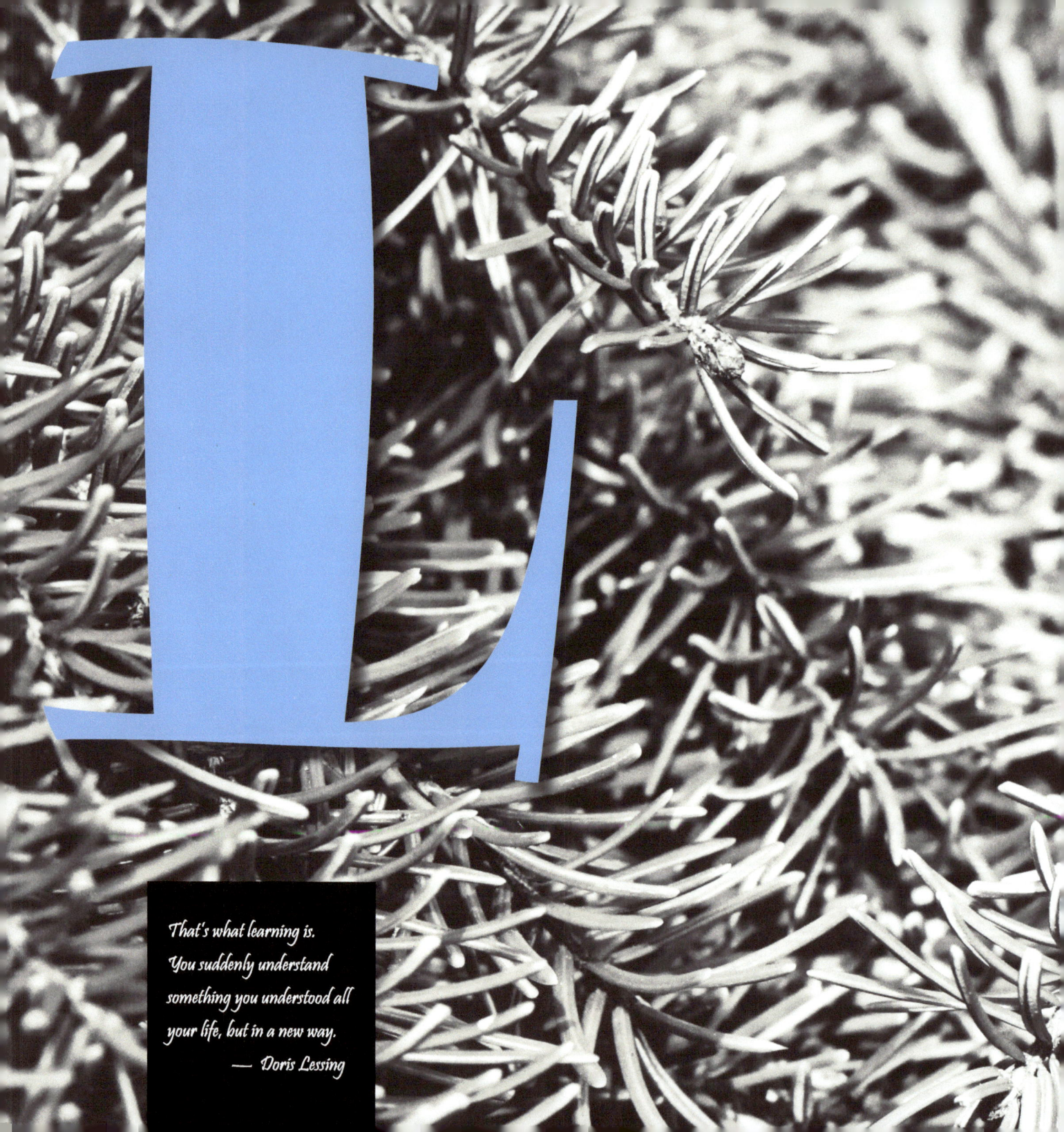

L

That's what learning is. You suddenly understand something you understood all your life, but in a new way.
— Doris Lessing

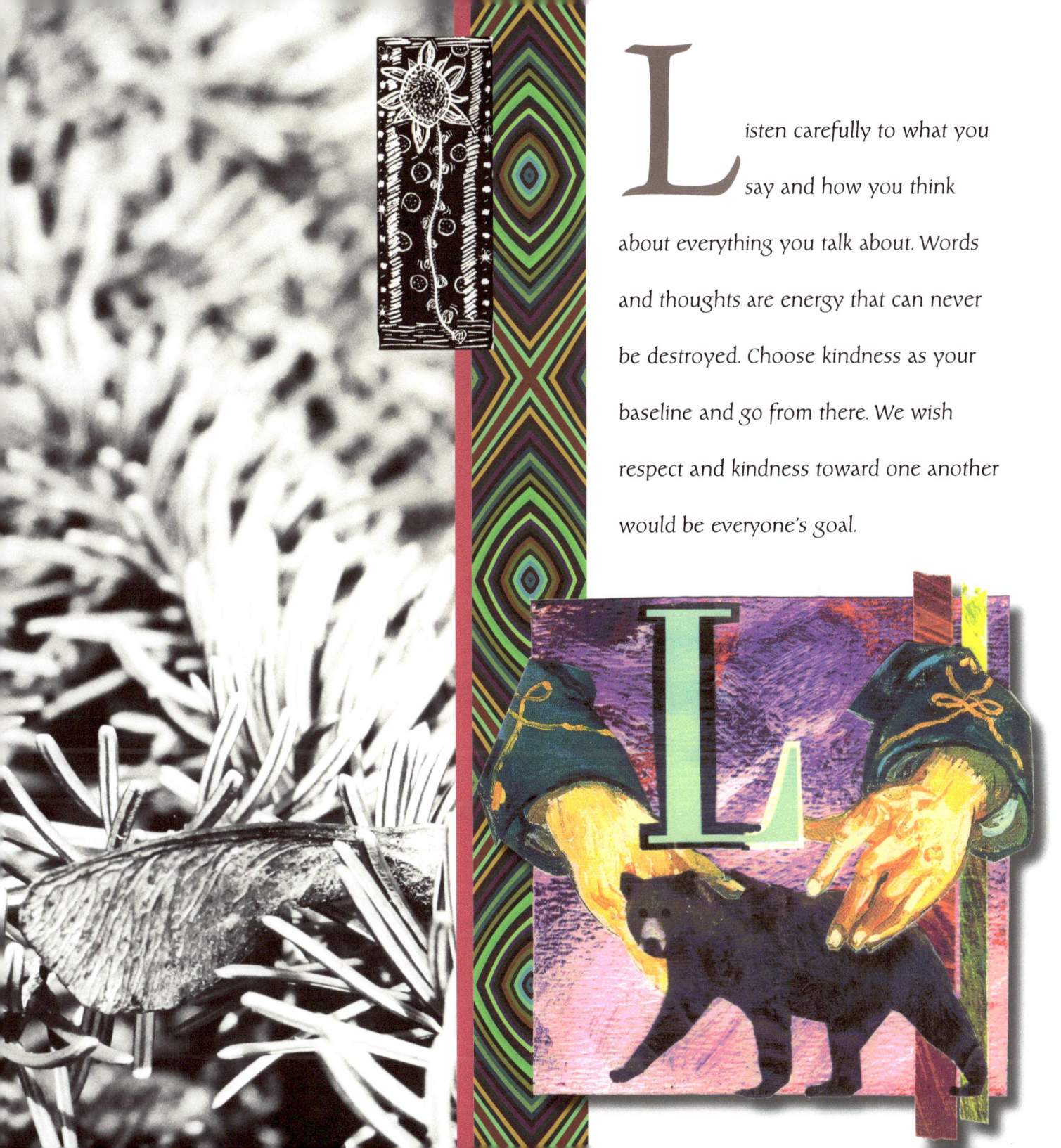

Listen carefully to what you say and how you think about everything you talk about. Words and thoughts are energy that can never be destroyed. Choose kindness as your baseline and go from there. We wish respect and kindness toward one another would be everyone's goal.

MAY THE BLESSINGS BE

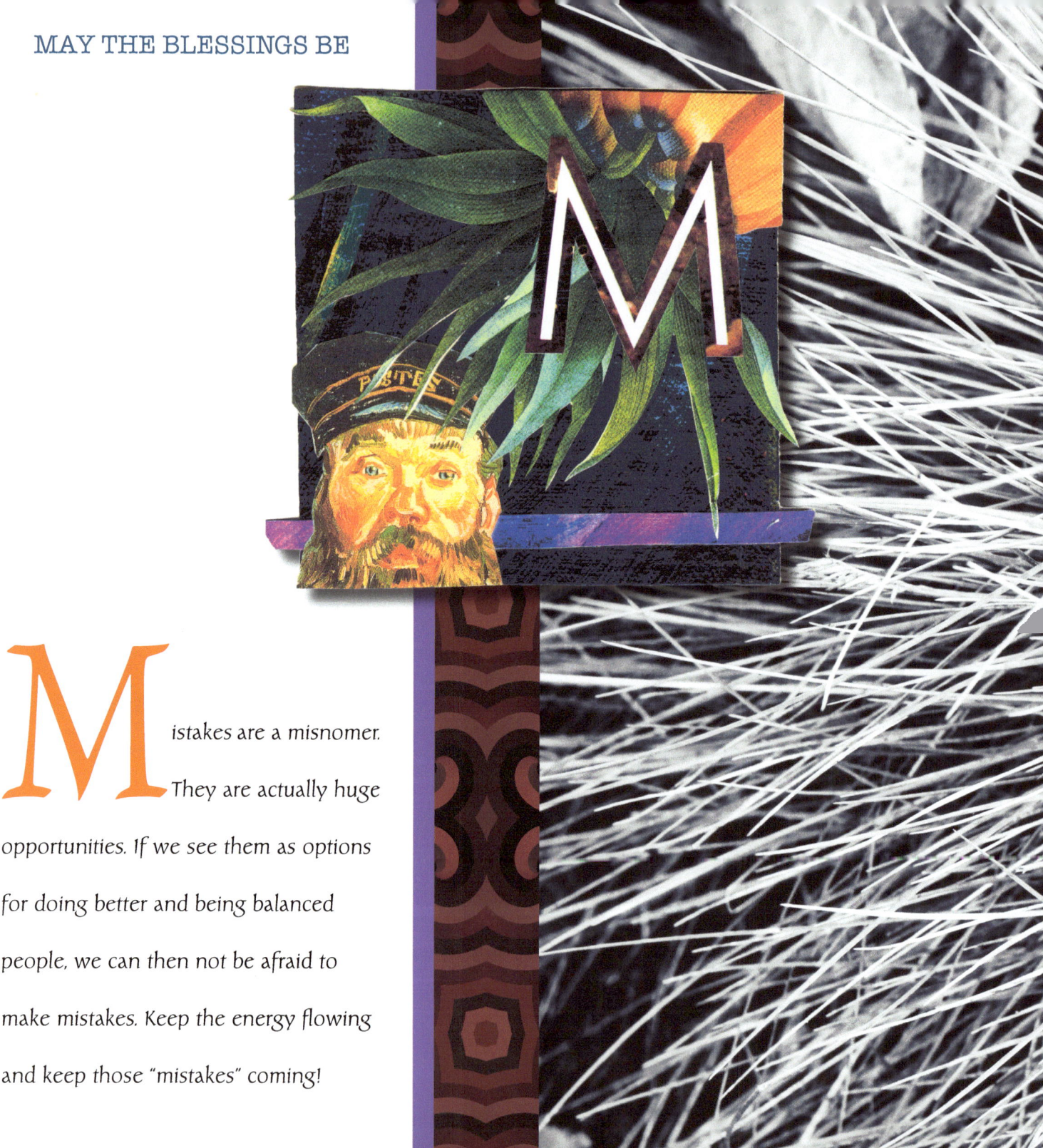

Mistakes are a misnomer. They are actually huge opportunities. If we see them as options for doing better and being balanced people, we can then not be afraid to make mistakes. Keep the energy flowing and keep those "mistakes" coming!

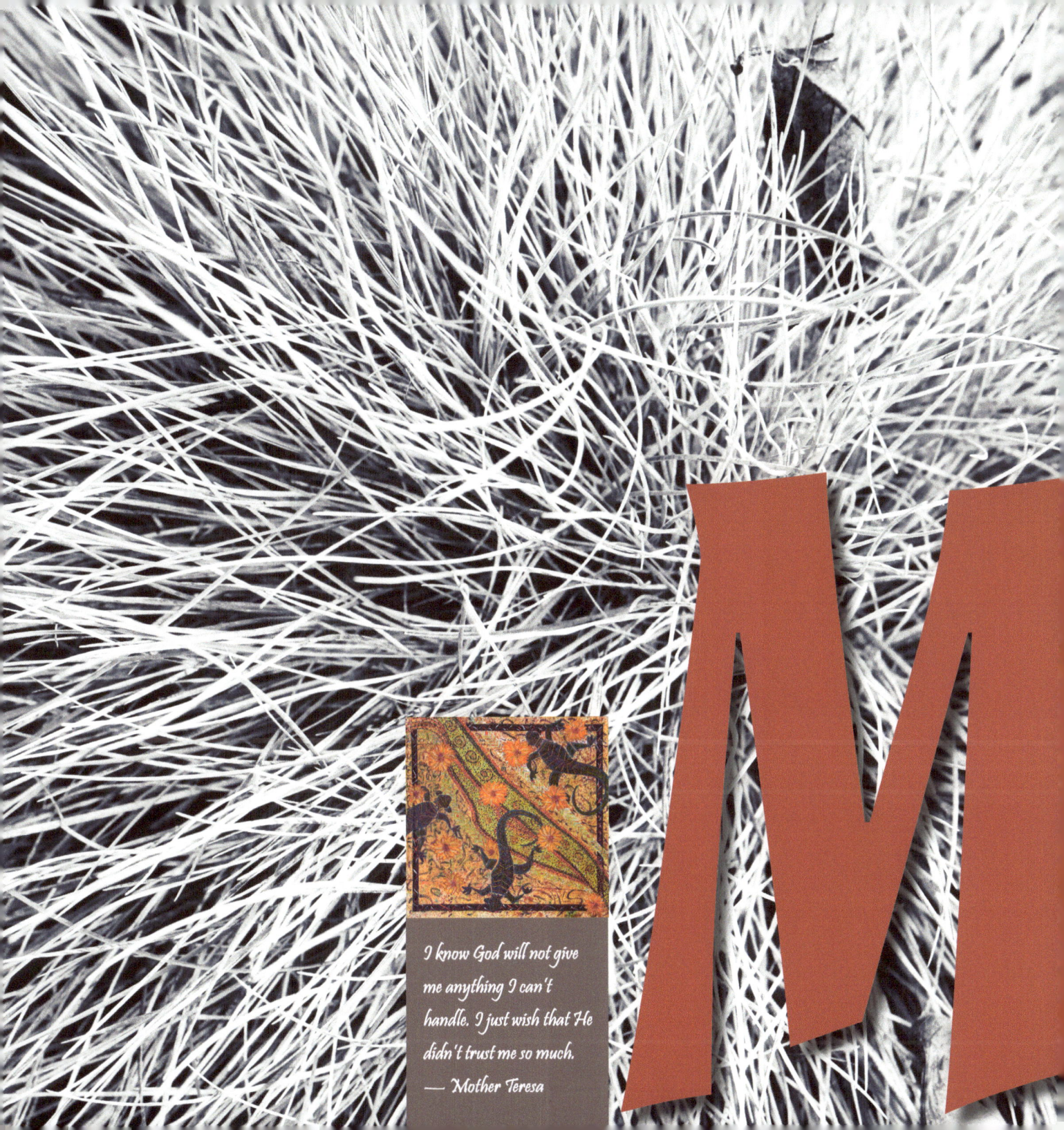

I know God will not give me anything I can't handle. I just wish that He didn't trust me so much.
— Mother Teresa

M

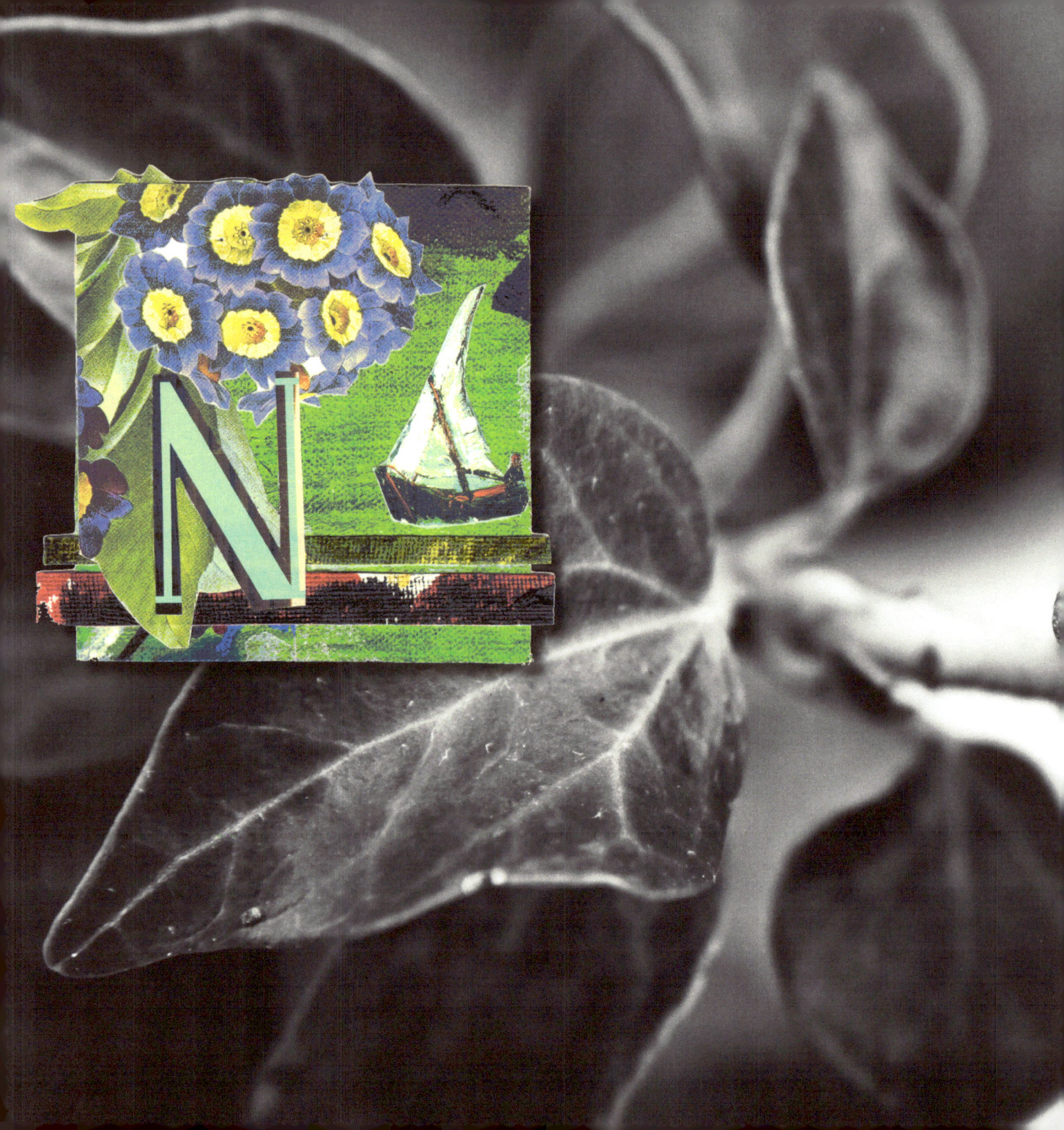

Our deepest fear is not that we are inadequate. Our deepest fear is that we are powerful beyond measure. It is our light, not our darkness, that most frightens us. Your playing small does not serve the world. There is nothing enlightened about shrinking so that other people won't feel insecure around you. We are all meant to shine as children do. It's not just in some of us; it is in everyone. And as we let our own lights shine, we unconsciously give other people permission to do the same. As we are liberated from our own fear, our presence automatically liberates others.
— Marianne Williamson

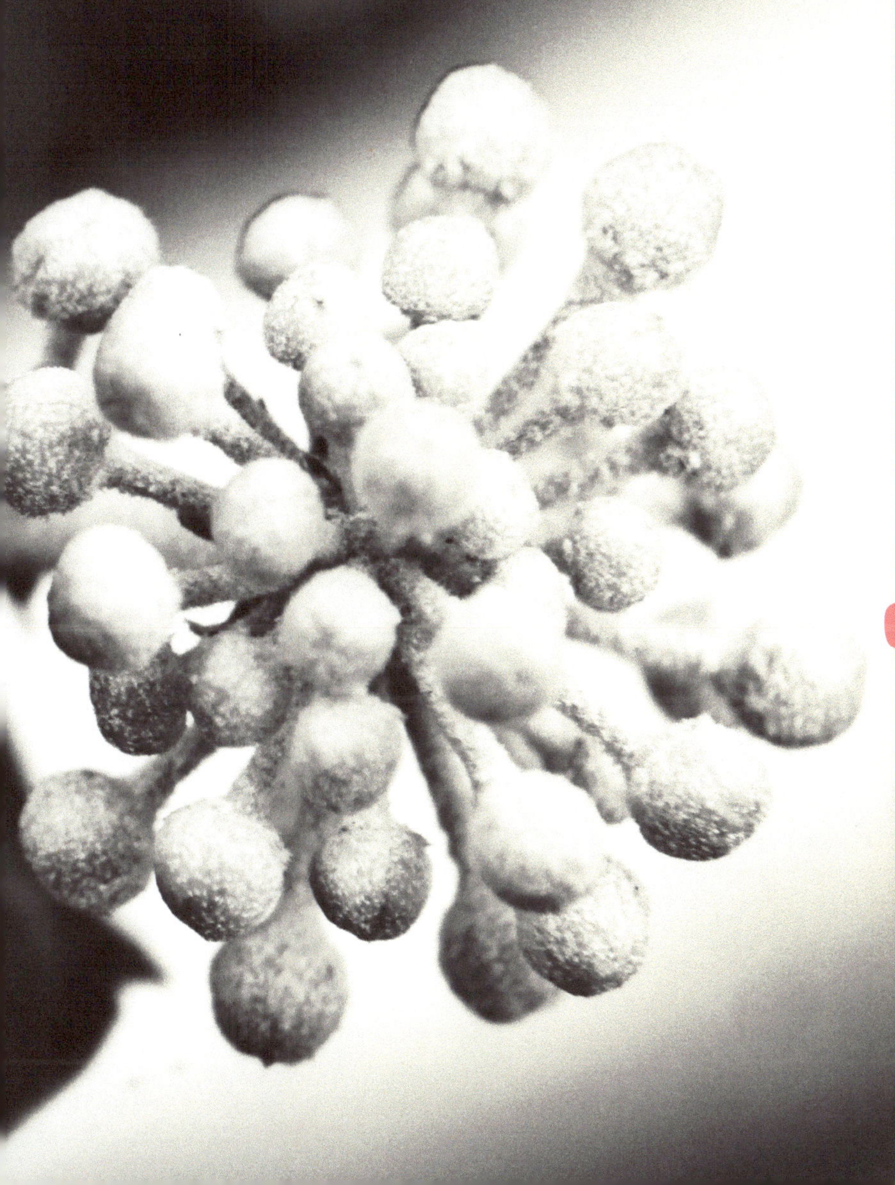

Now, this very minute, this very second, is the only time there is. The past is the past and the future does not exist. It is what you do with the now that makes the difference. Your intuition, that gut feeling we often ignore, will tell you the direction to move in. Trust it now.

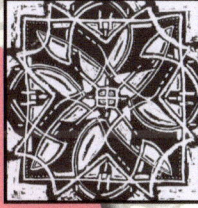

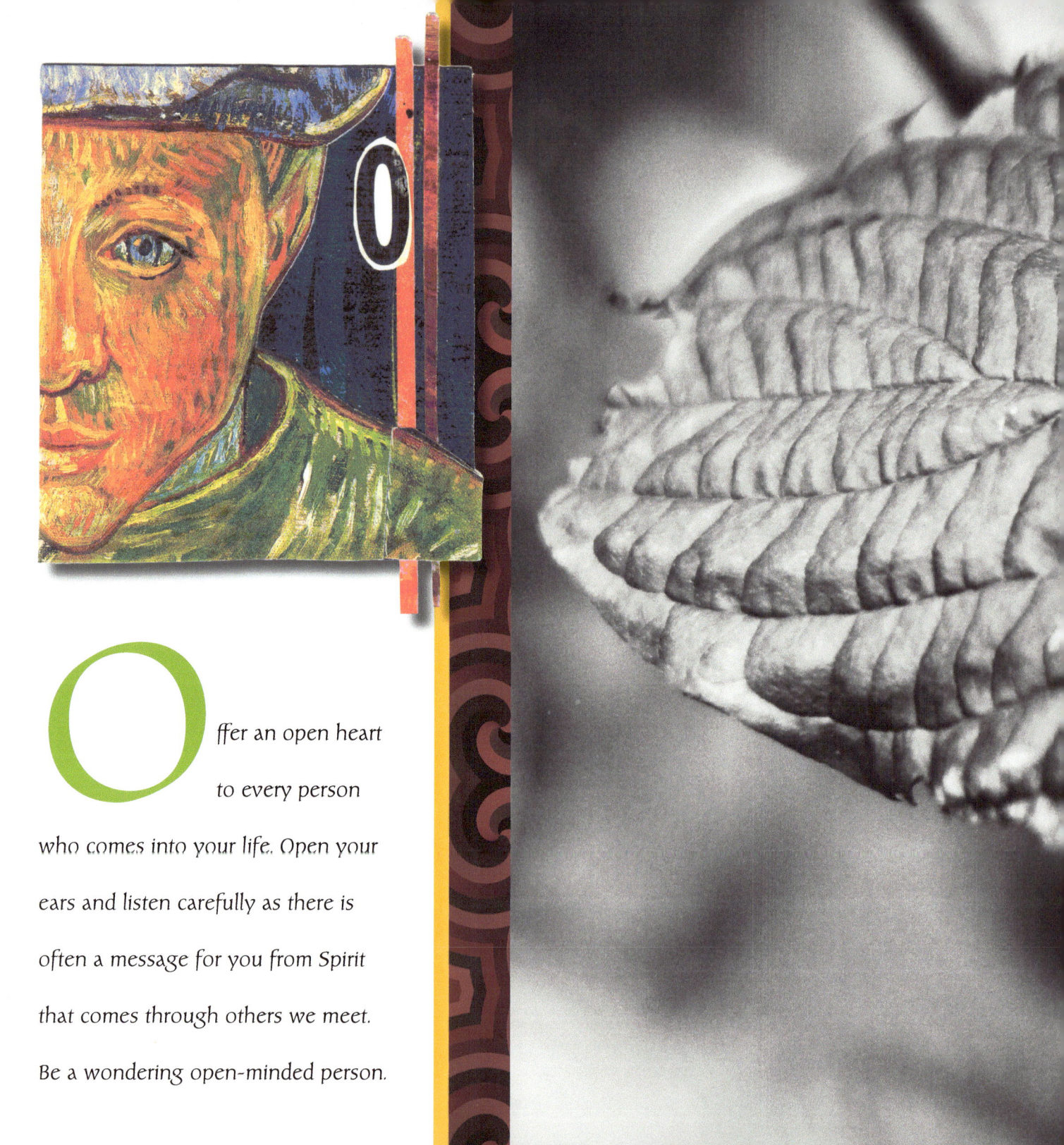

Offer an open heart to every person who comes into your life. Open your ears and listen carefully as there is often a message for you from Spirit that comes through others we meet. Be a wondering open-minded person.

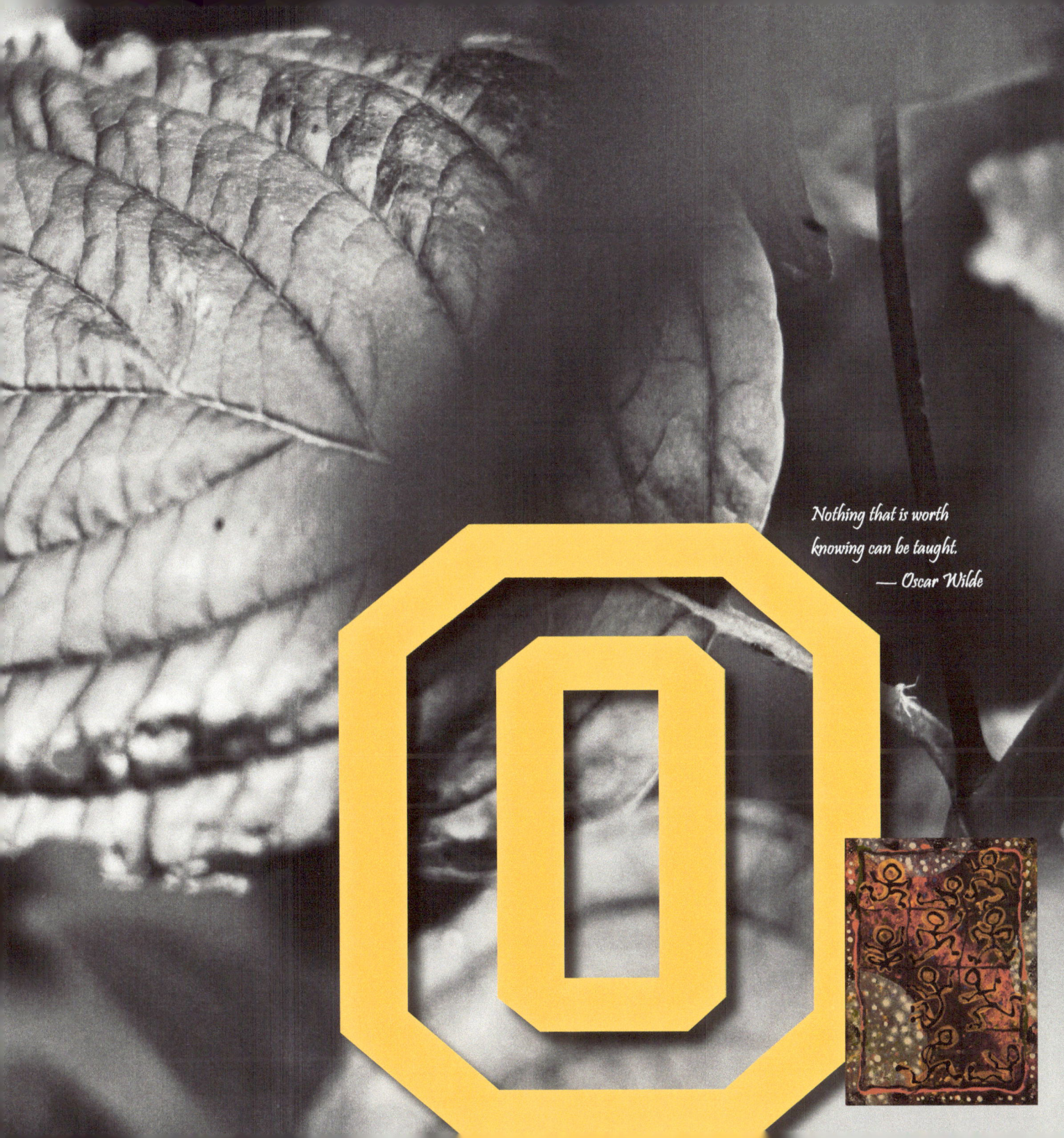

Nothing that is worth knowing can be taught.
— *Oscar Wilde*

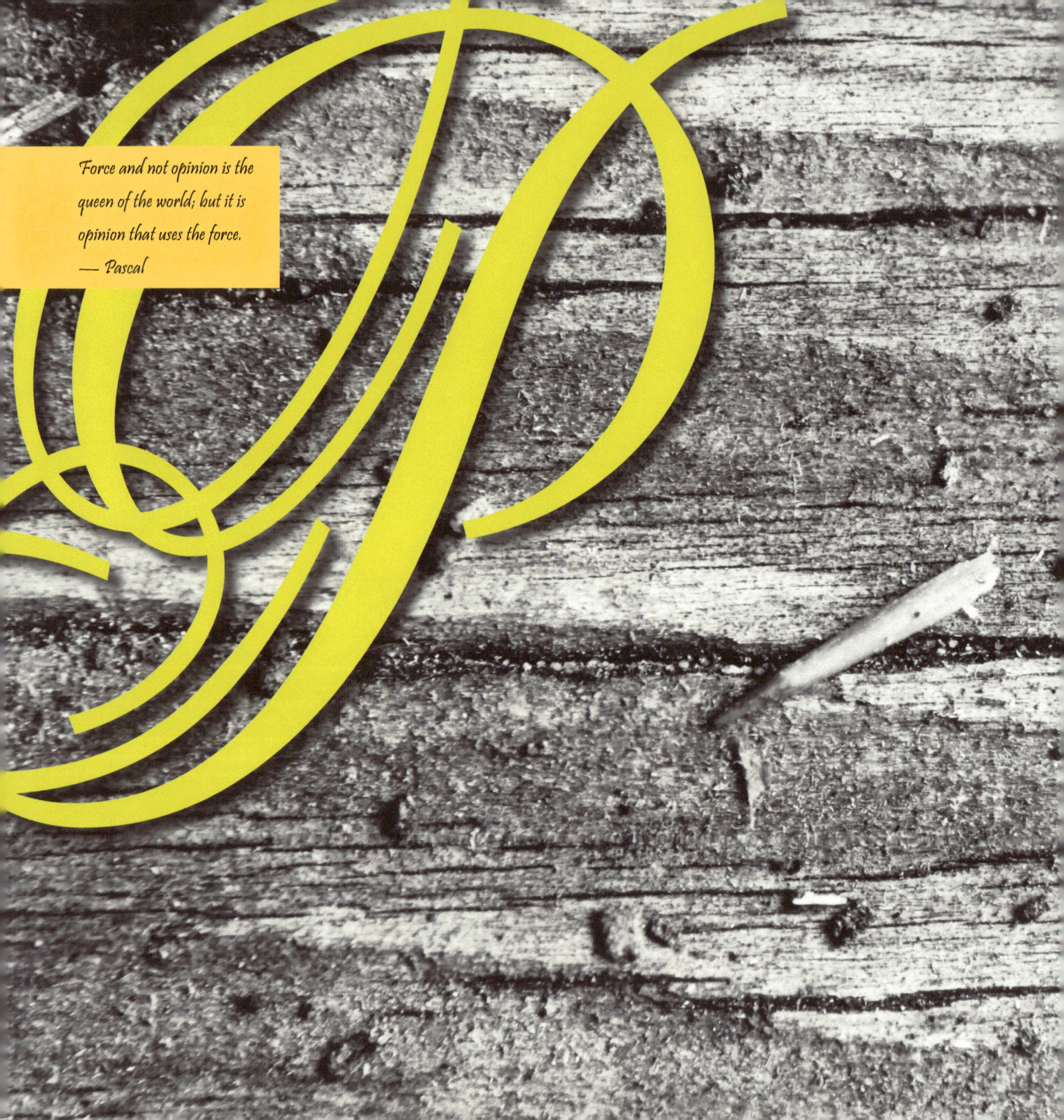

> Force and not opinion is the queen of the world; but it is opinion that uses the force.
> — Pascal

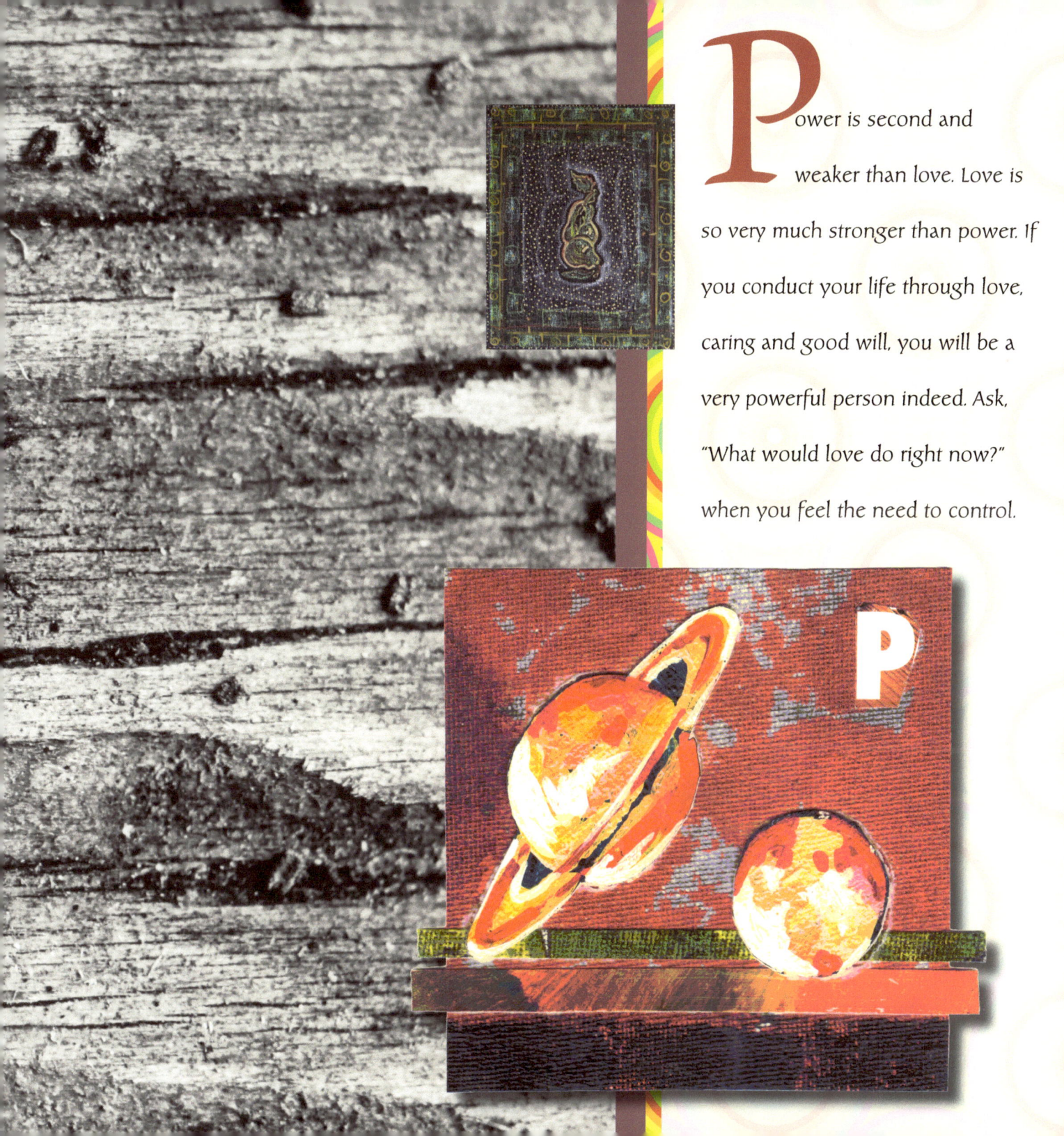

Power is second and weaker than love. Love is so very much stronger than power. If you conduct your life through love, caring and good will, you will be a very powerful person indeed. Ask, "What would love do right now?" when you feel the need to control.

Quiet in body, mind and thought is necessary everyday so that we can hear the life stream speak to us. The Earth's pace of life is so fast that we must take time to listen to the directions and options that are being offered to us from Divine Energy for our own growth and well being. Sit and contemplate — we are surrounded by miracles.

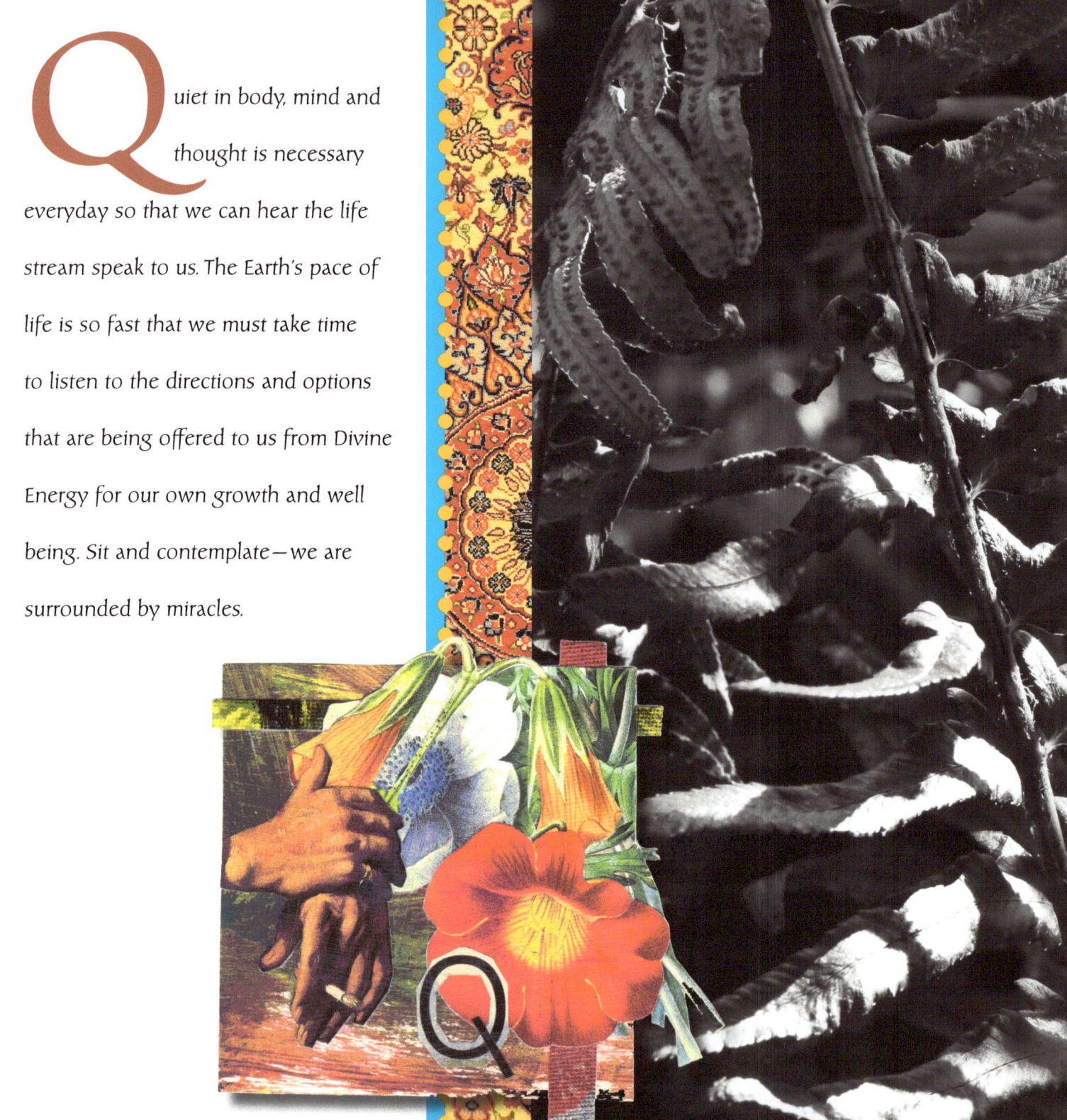

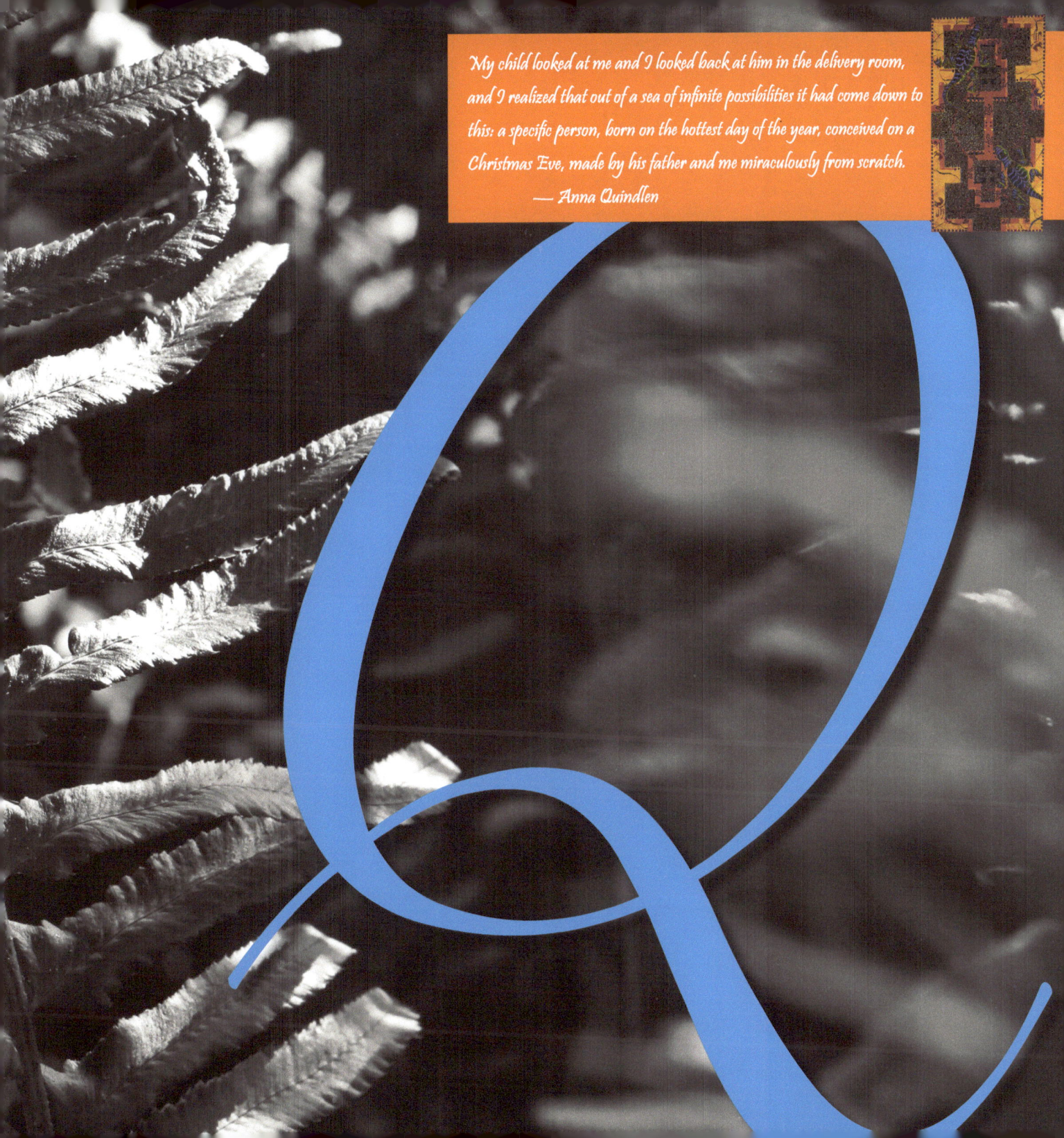

My child looked at me and I looked back at him in the delivery room, and I realized that out of a sea of infinite possibilities it had come down to this: a specific person, born on the hottest day of the year, conceived on a Christmas Eve, made by his father and me miraculously from scratch.
— Anna Quindlen

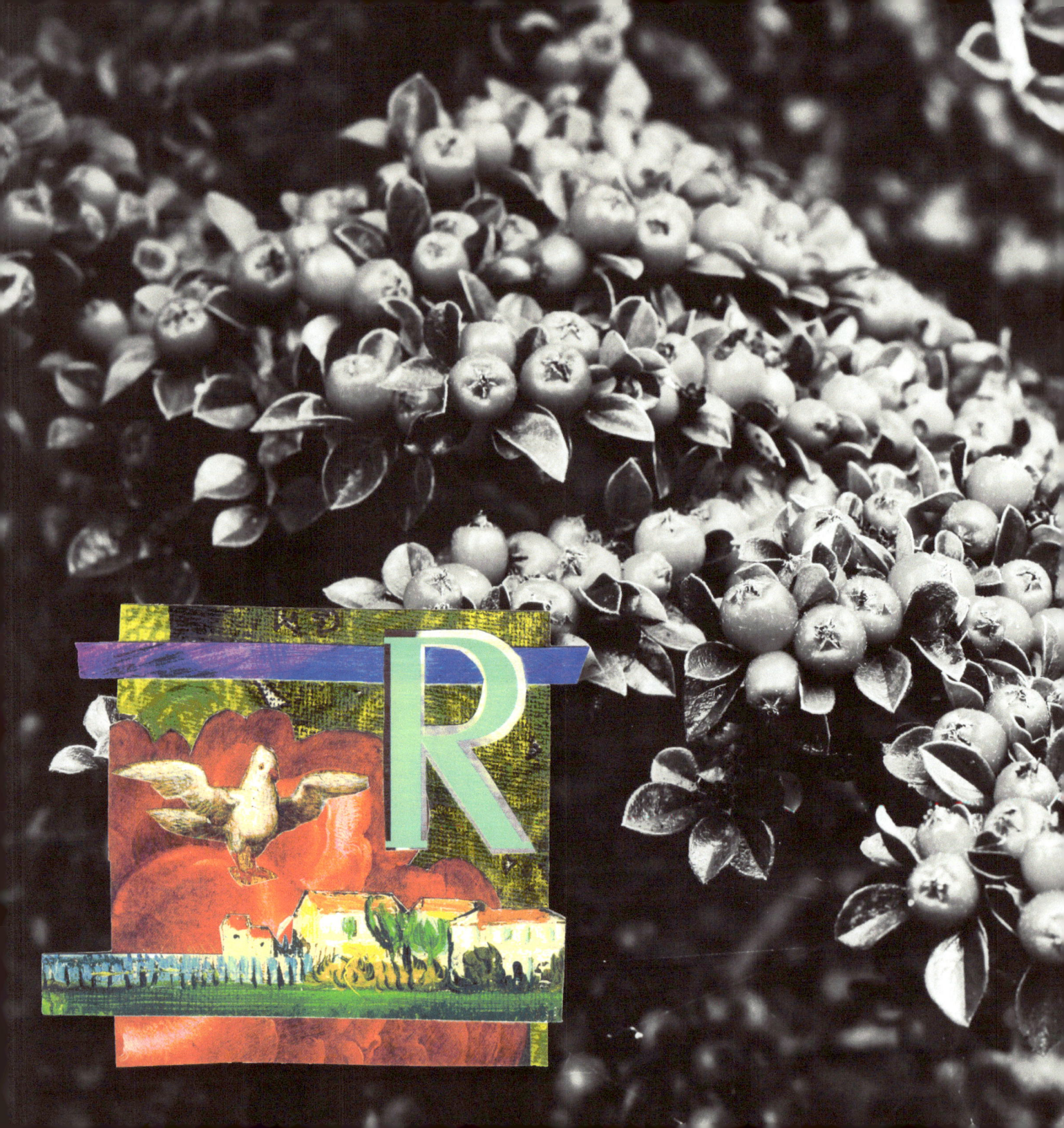

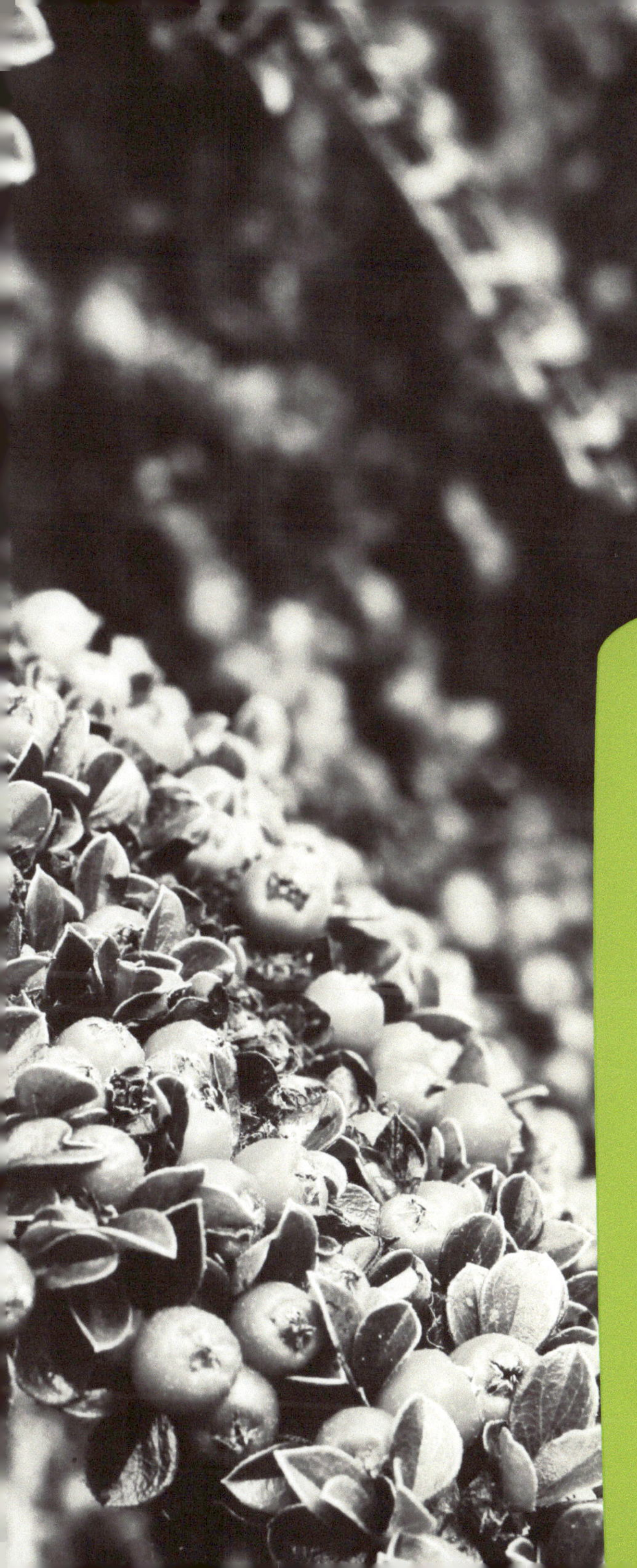

R eflections—if we are challenged with how we perceive others' behaviours, remember that we can only see in others what they mirror-back to us of our own behaviour. If someone's actions bother you, ask "When do I do this?" Then take note and reflect. Maybe even thank them silently.

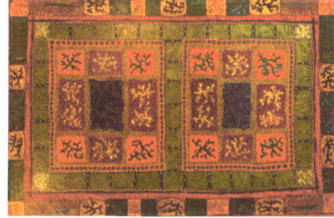

Do not go where the path may lead, go instead where there is no path and leave a trail.
— *Ralph Waldo Emerson*

Stop trying to figure everything out. All is as it is suppose to be. Accept it all, including yourself. Is the cup half-full or half-empty? Or could it be holding exactly what we need and want? Stop thinking there is an answer that will explain everything. Accept whatever is at hand as what the next step is suppose to be. Embrace the task and relax into it.

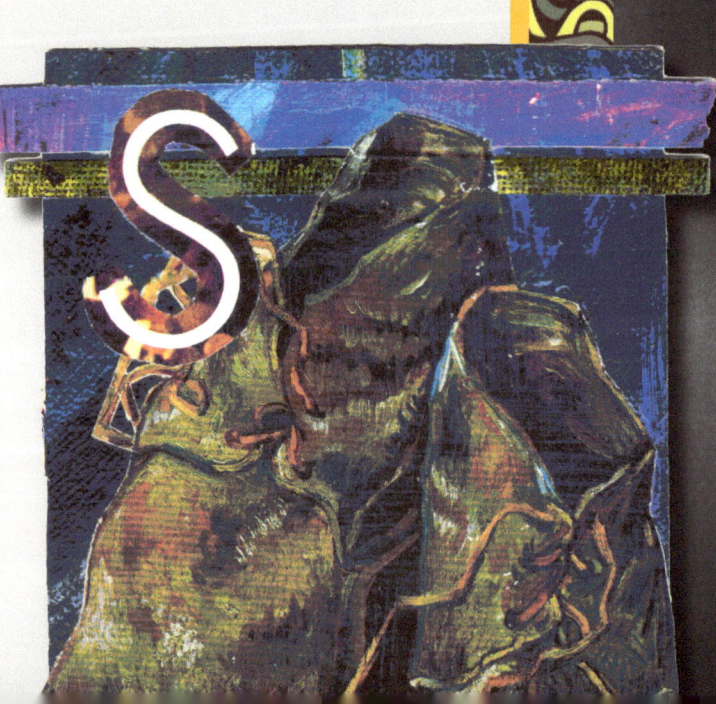

As a kid, you see something that you know in your heart is true. It's such a huge hypocrisy that it makes you think,, "Well, if this is a truth that I know about that's not officially accepted, at least in this country, then how many other truths are there that are under the surface that need to come out?"
— Serj Tankian

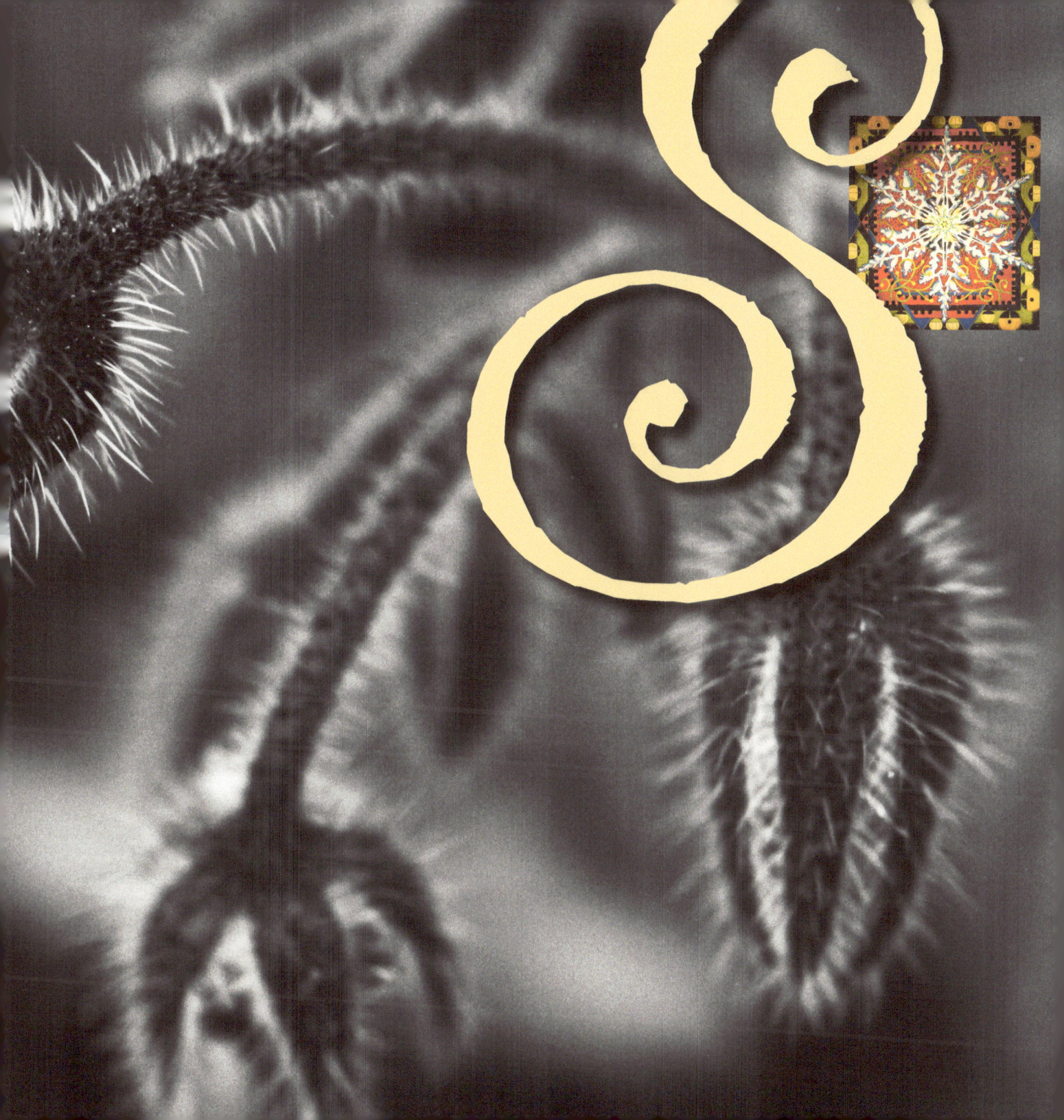

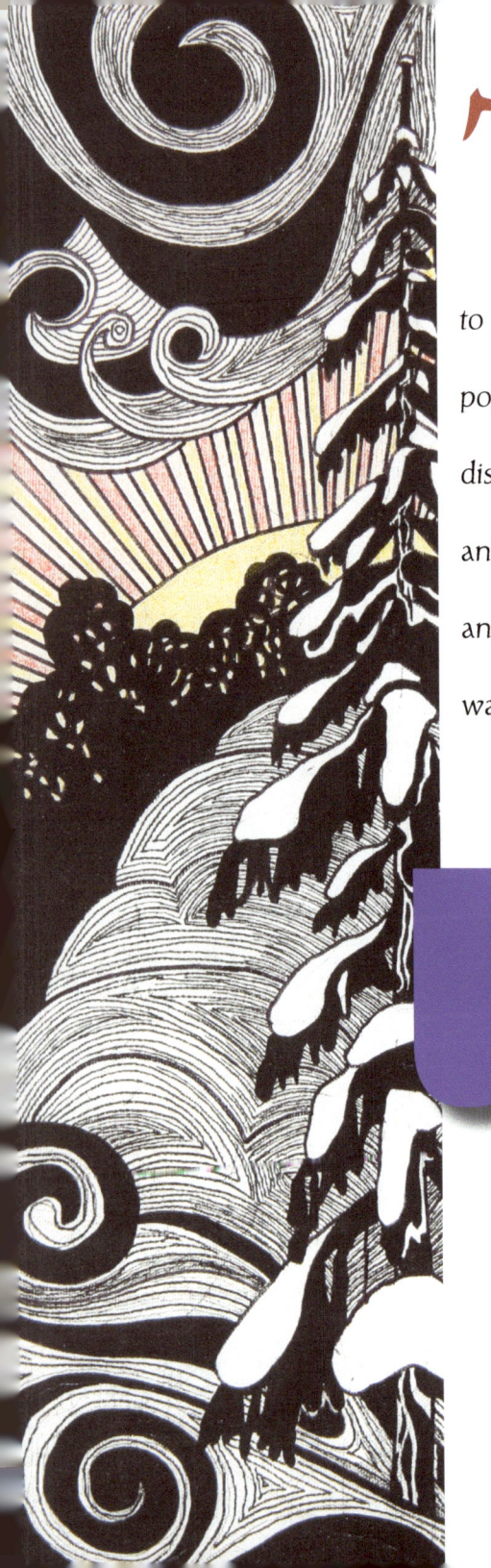

Truth is different for each of us. There is no need to seek truth—just stop having points of view. Do not agree or disagree, do not adopt or reject anything. Keep a totally open mind and see what truth comes your way. It'll always be interesting.

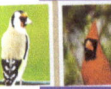

An association of men who will not quarrel with one another is a thing which has never yet existed, from the greatest confederacy of nations down to a town meeting or a vestry.
— Thomas Jefferson

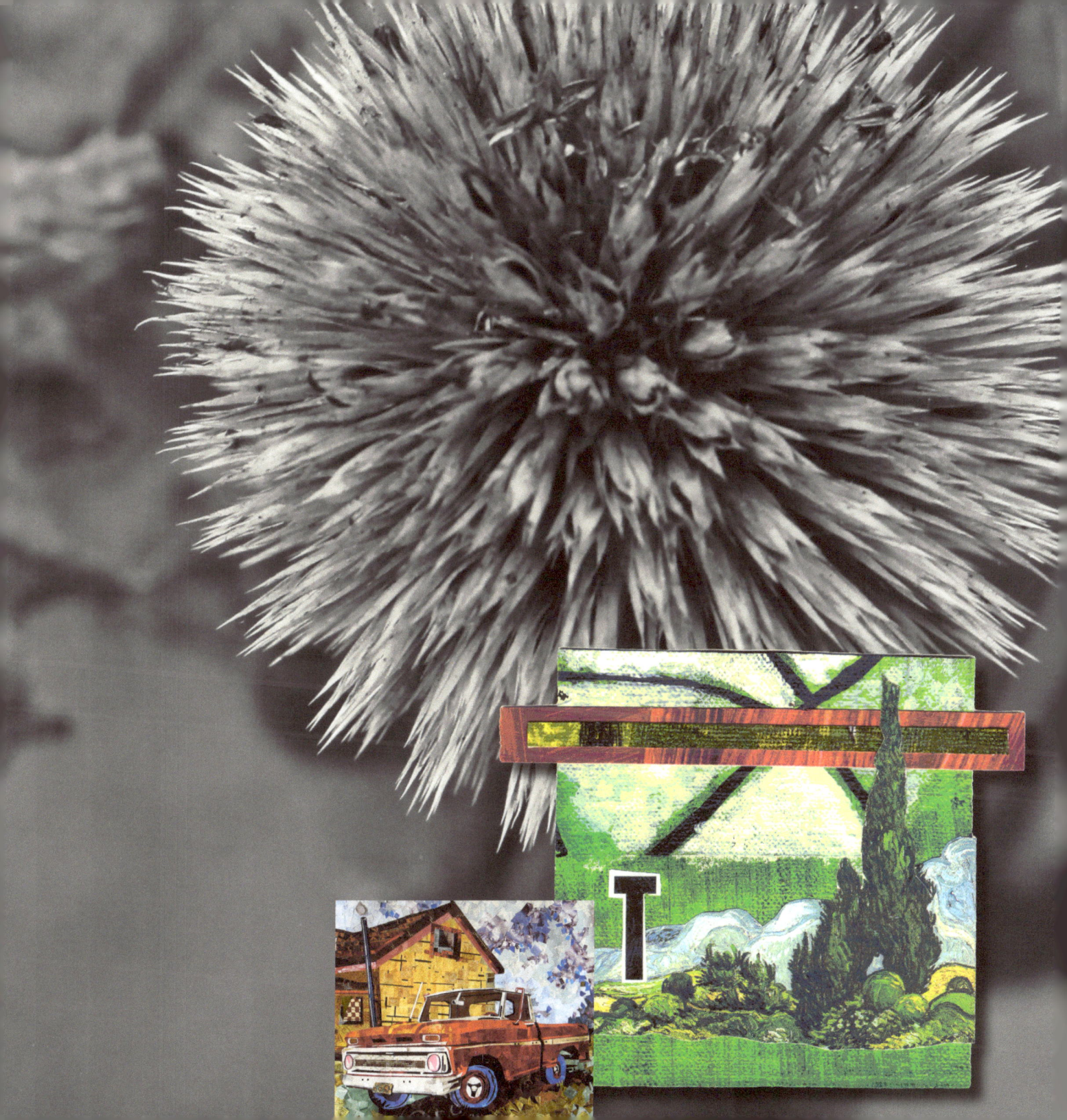

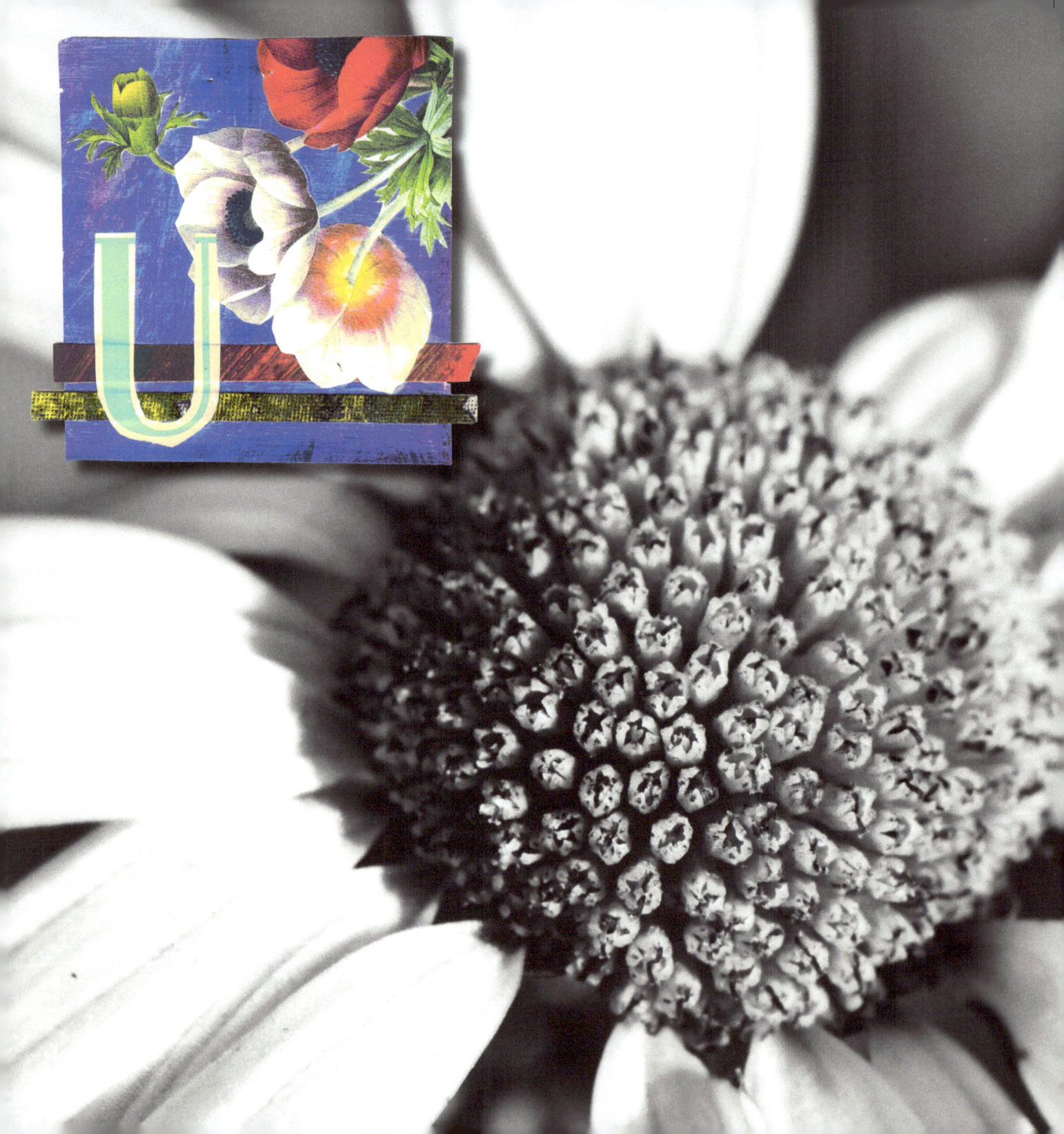

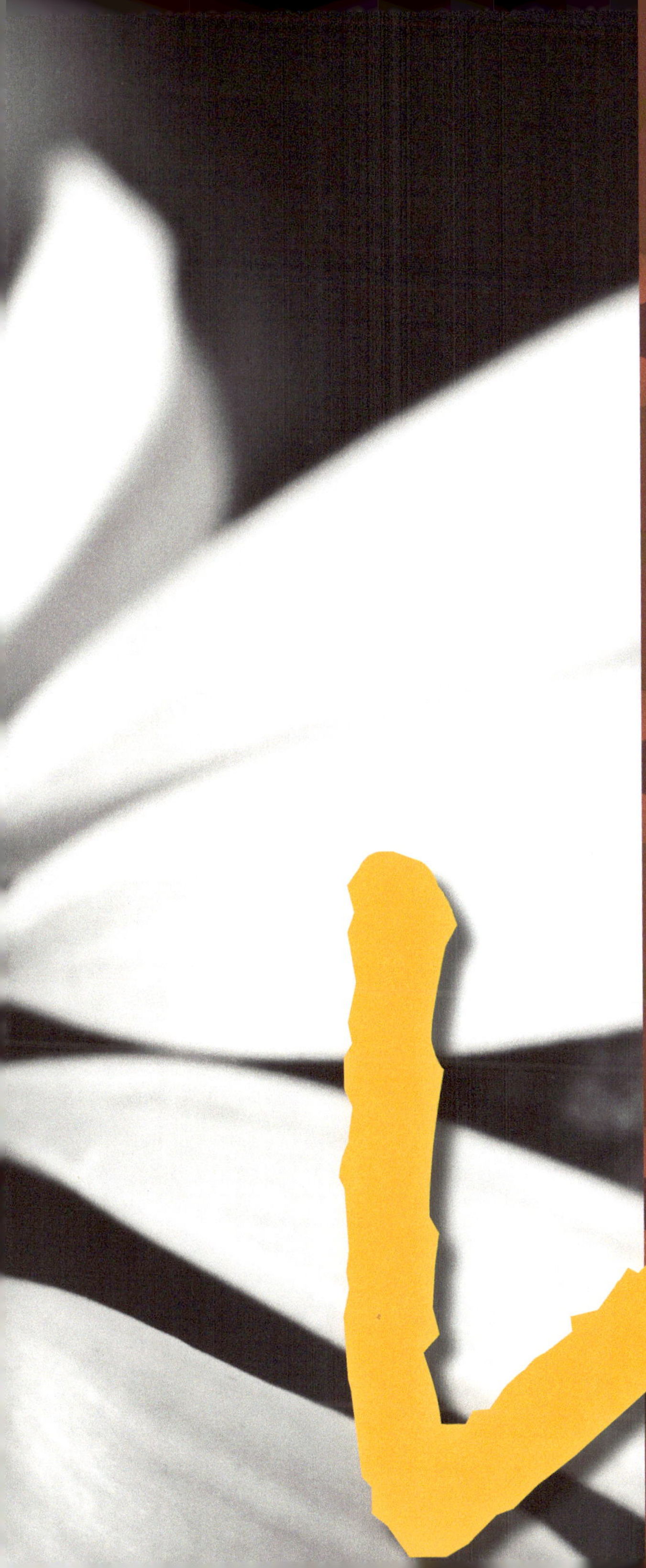

Unexpected opportunities are around every corner of life. By staying open, non-judgmental and neutral we will be able to see, accept and use these blessings that are being given to us from the stream of life. Listen carefully because life speaks to us all personally every minute of every day. The ultimate gift!

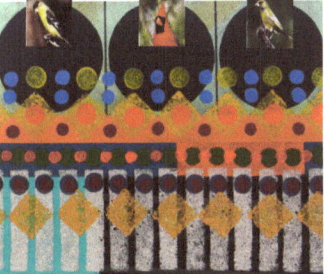

Happiness is to be found along the way, not at the end of the road, for then the journey is over and it is too late. Today, this hour, this minute is the day, the hour, the minute for each of us to sense the fact that life is good, with all of its trials and troubles, and perhaps more interesting because of them.
— *Robert R. Updegraff*

The progress of rivers to the ocean is not so rapid as that of man to error.
— Voltaire

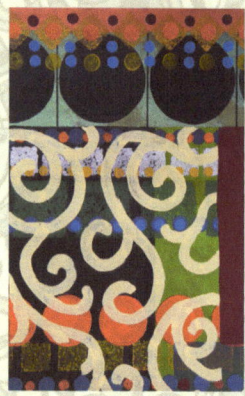

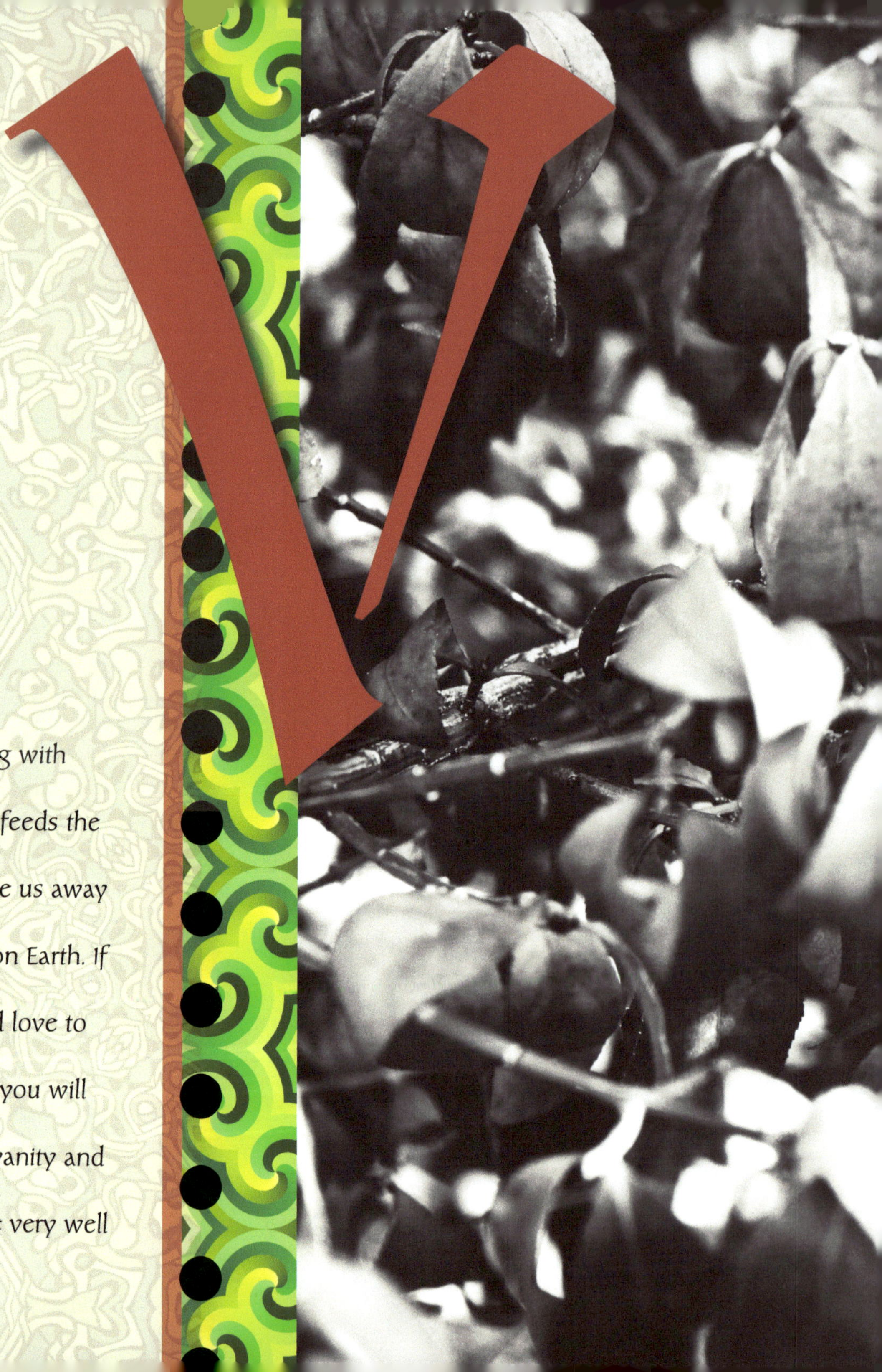

Vanity is a trap. Along with greed and anger, it feeds the Ego. Ego's only job is to confuse us away from what really matters here on Earth. If you live by offering service and love to everyone you know and meet, you will find your way. Get away from vanity and Ego, be humble and you will be very well looked after.

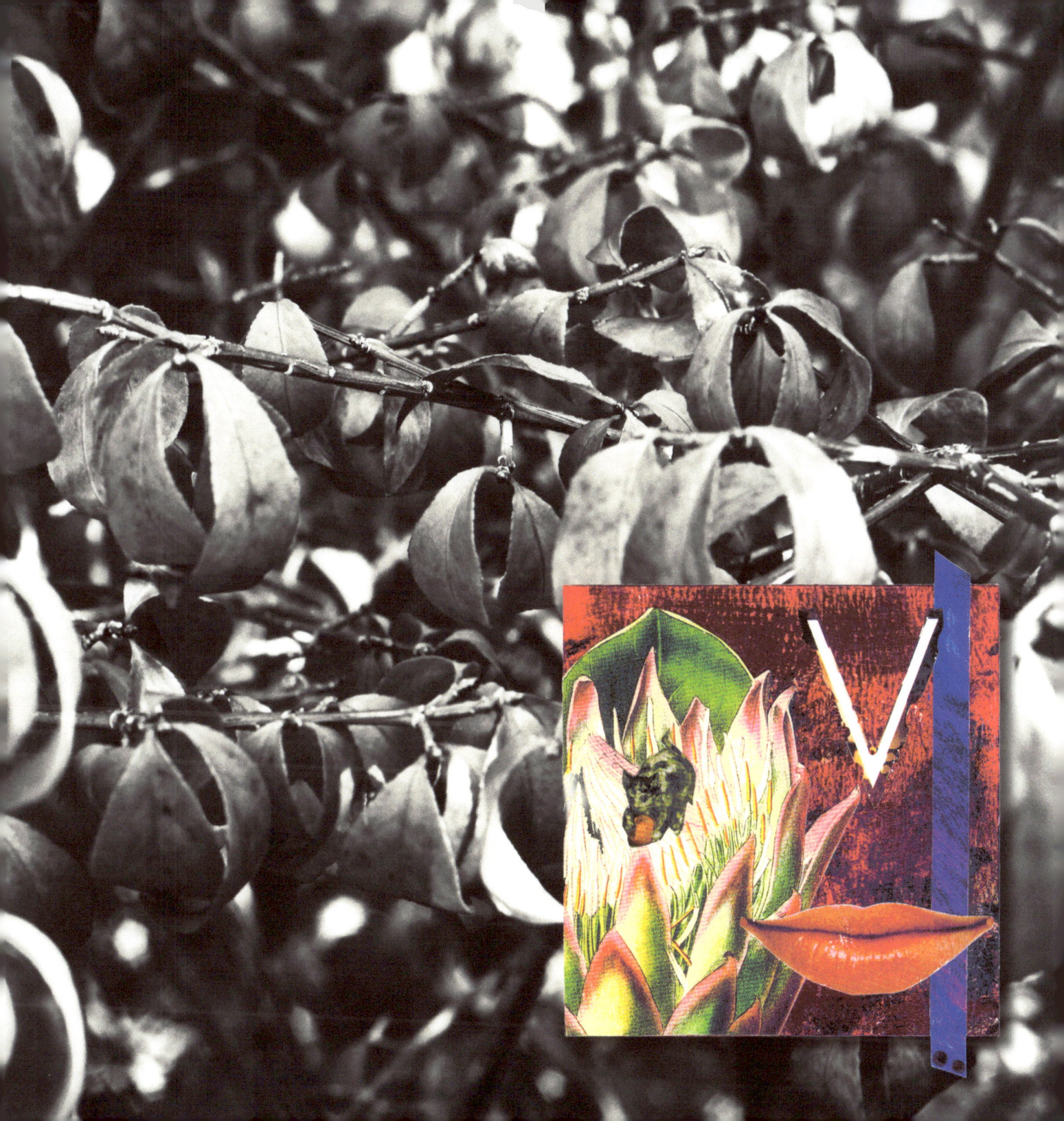

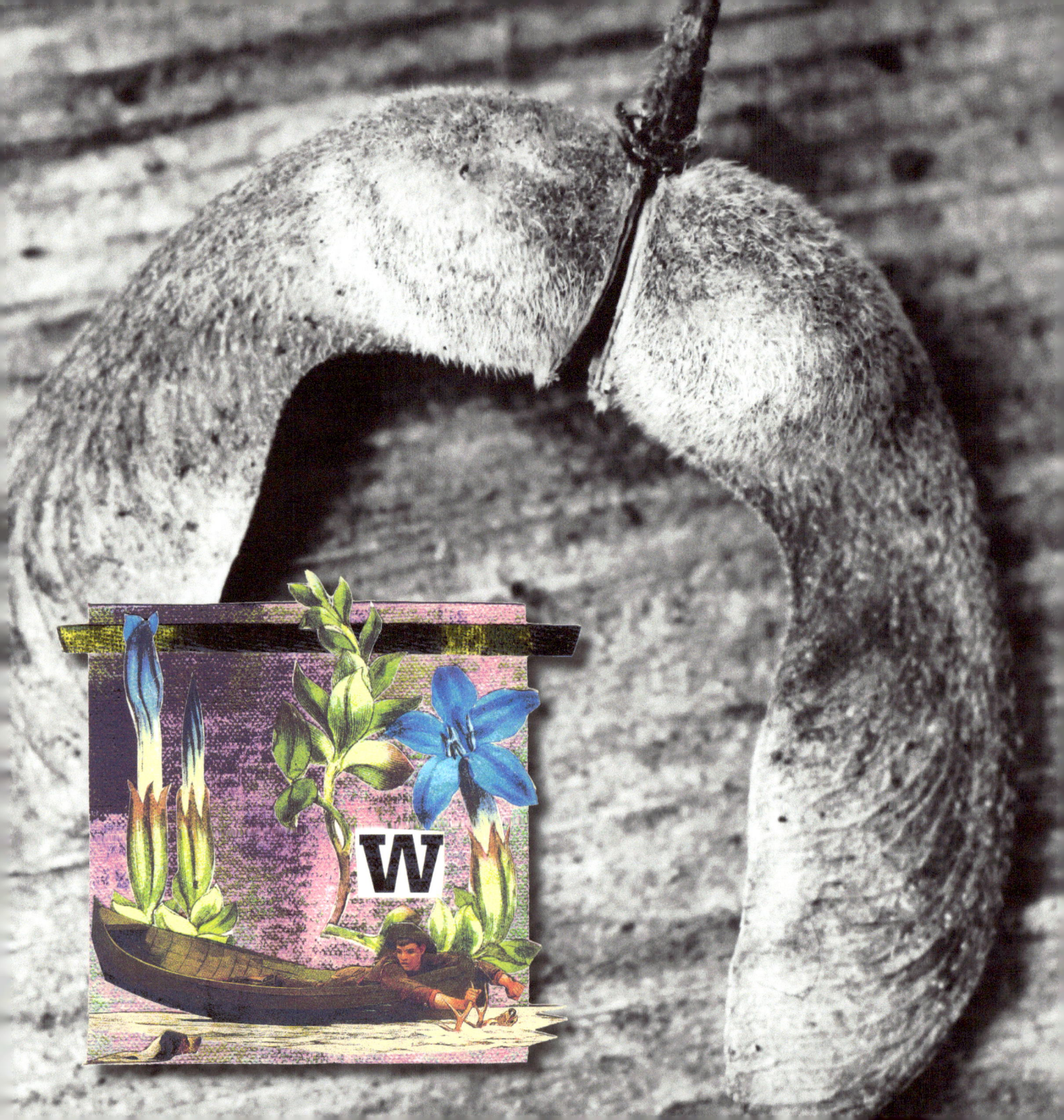

> *No folly is more costly than the folly of intolerant idealism.*
> — *Winston Churchill*

We must leave others just as we've found them because they have their own path and lessons to live. Interfering in their life only creates more karmic problems for both of you. We can only change ourselves and our own points of view. If they ask for help that is another matter—offer your ideas while expecting nothing.

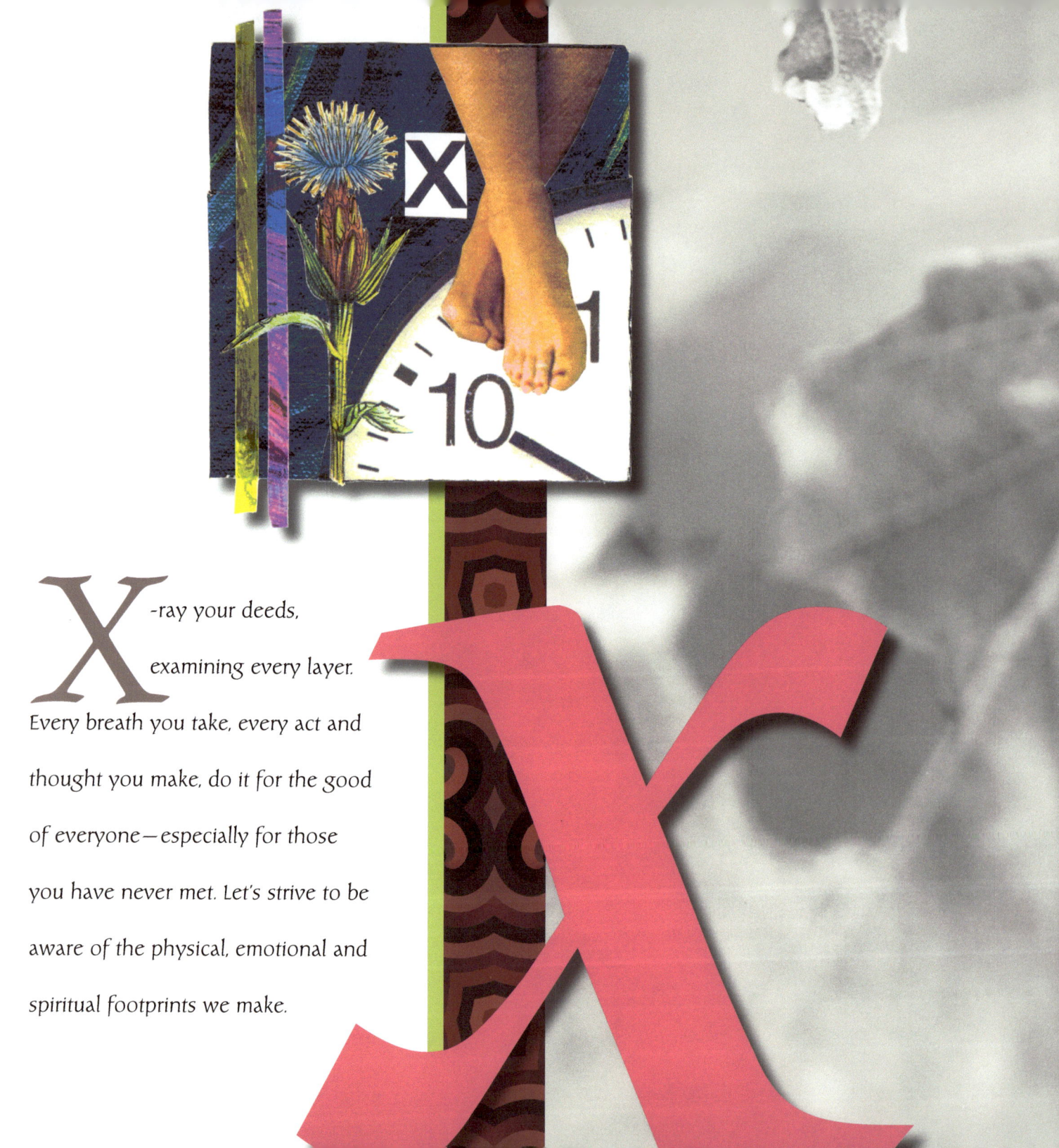

X-ray your deeds, examining every layer. Every breath you take, every act and thought you make, do it for the good of everyone—especially for those you have never met. Let's strive to be aware of the physical, emotional and spiritual footprints we make.

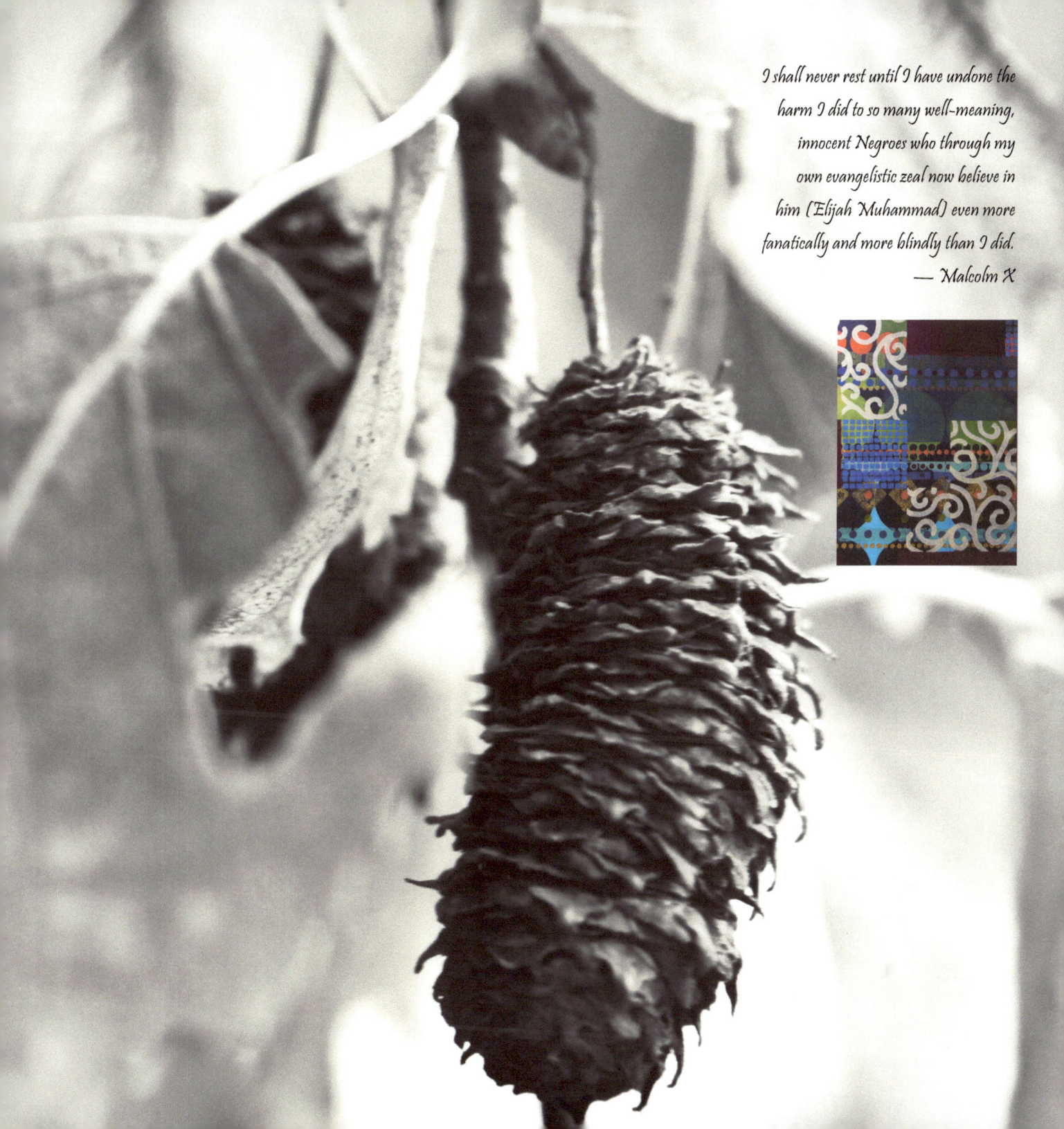

I shall never rest until I have undone the harm I did to so many well-meaning, innocent Negroes who through my own evangelistic zeal now believe in him (Elijah Muhammad) even more fanatically and more blindly than I did.
— Malcolm X

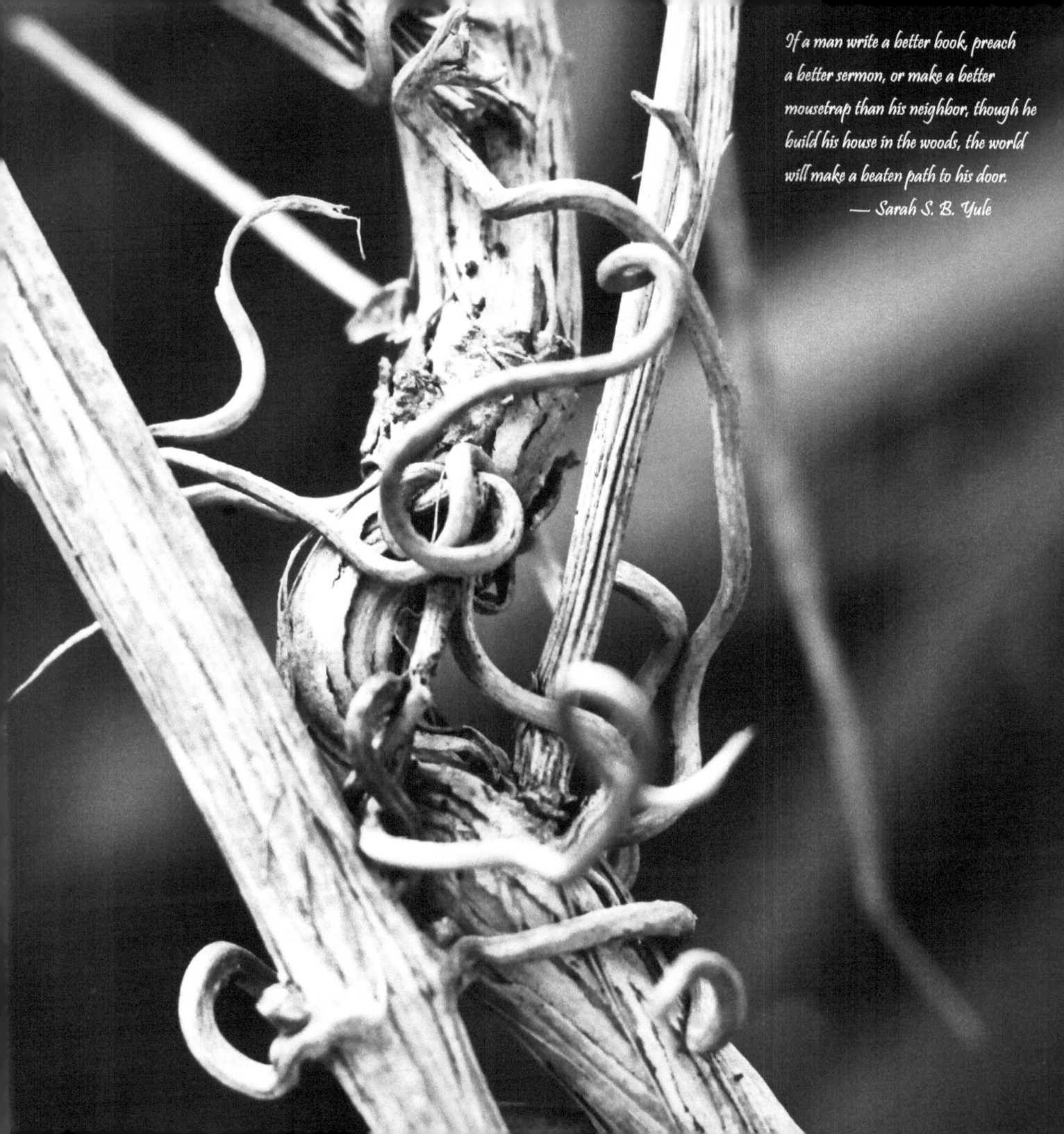

> If a man write a better book, preach a better sermon, or make a better mousetrap than his neighbor, though he build his house in the woods, the world will make a beaten path to his door.
> — Sarah S. B. Yule

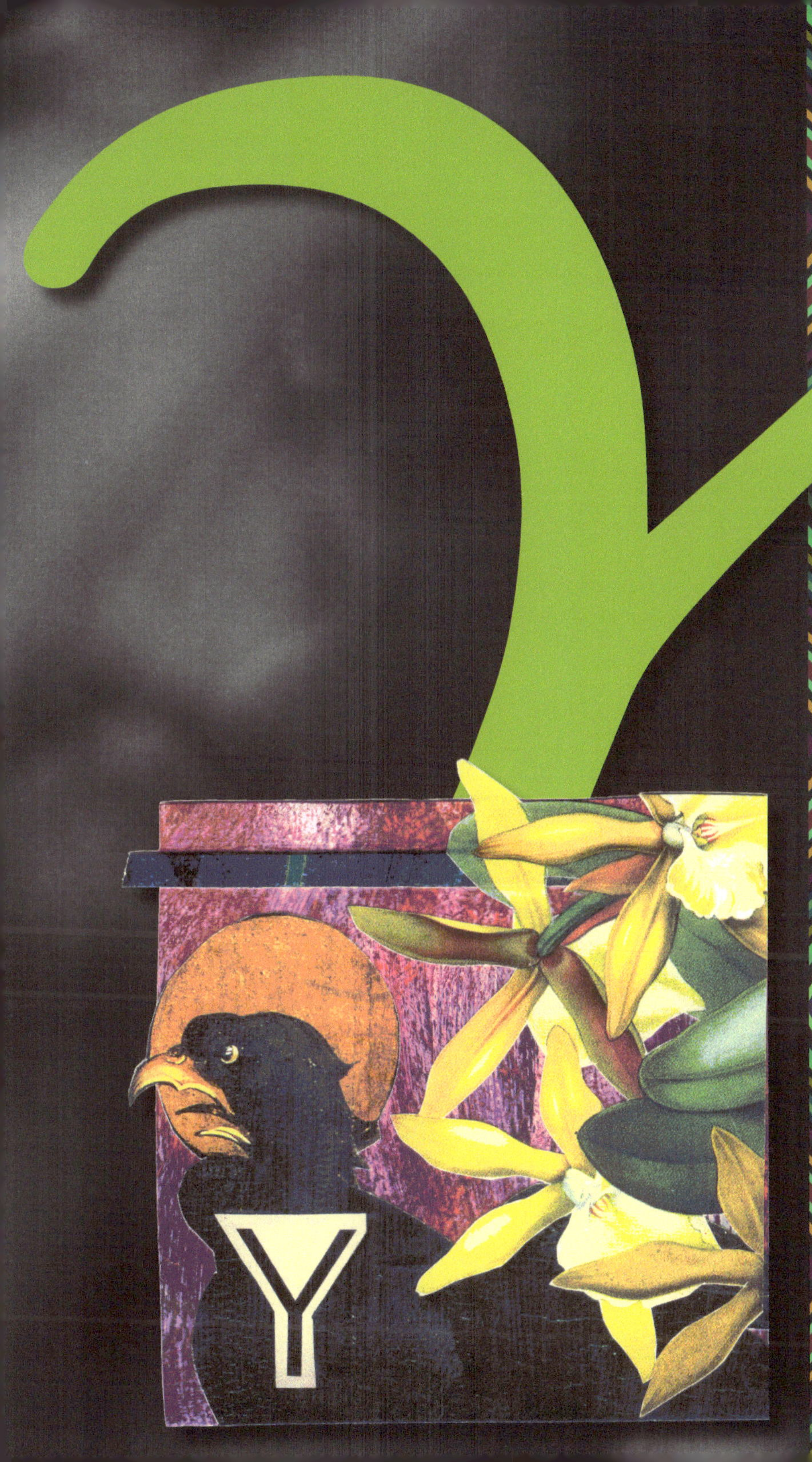

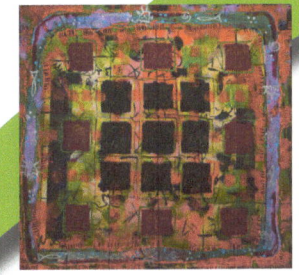

You are a Soul having an Earthly experience, living in a physical body. If you keep that body clean, fit and healthy you will be able to receive all that you've earned and you wanted to learn while being here. With a healthy body, our mind and spirit are clearer to respond… and to play!

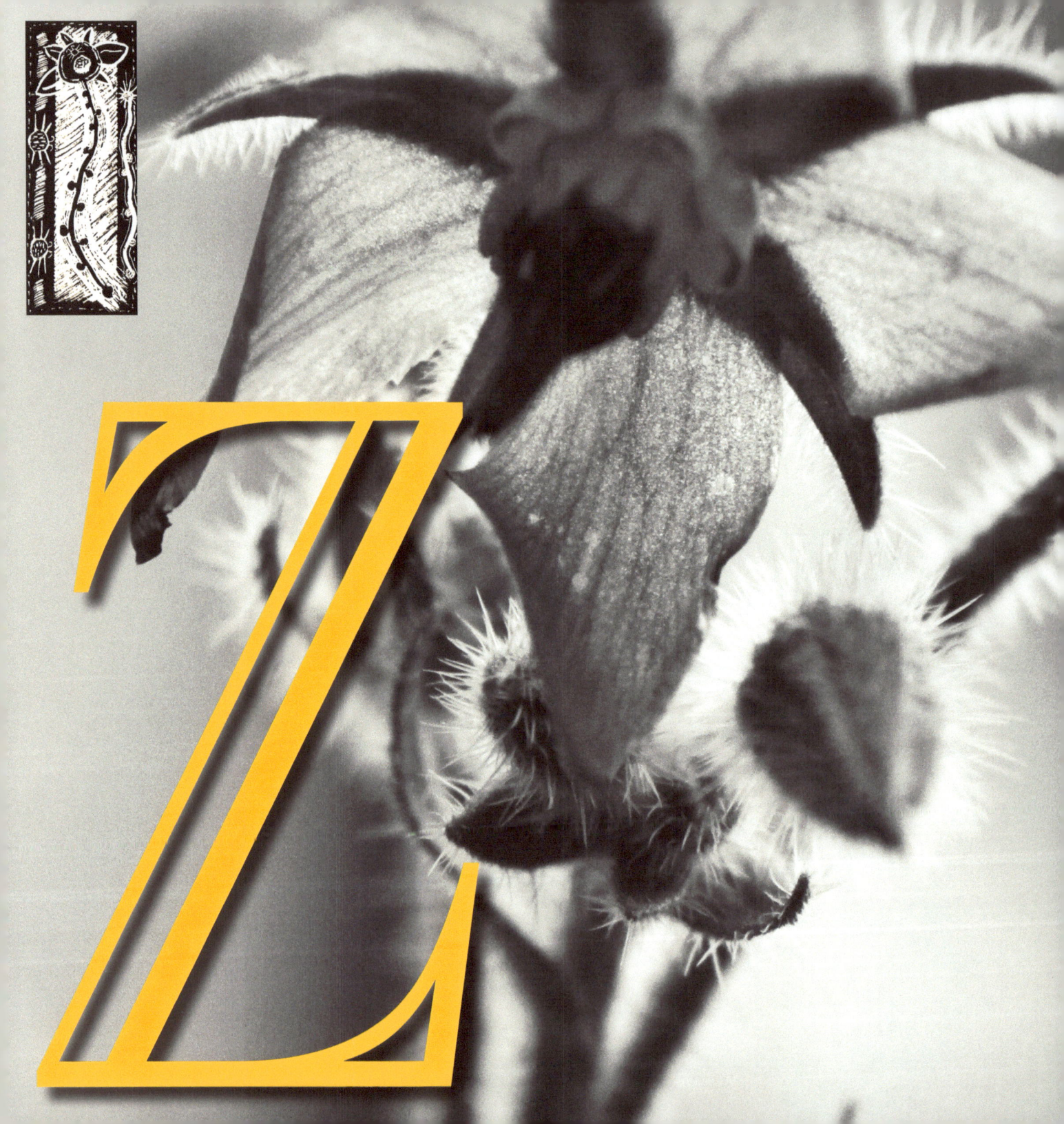

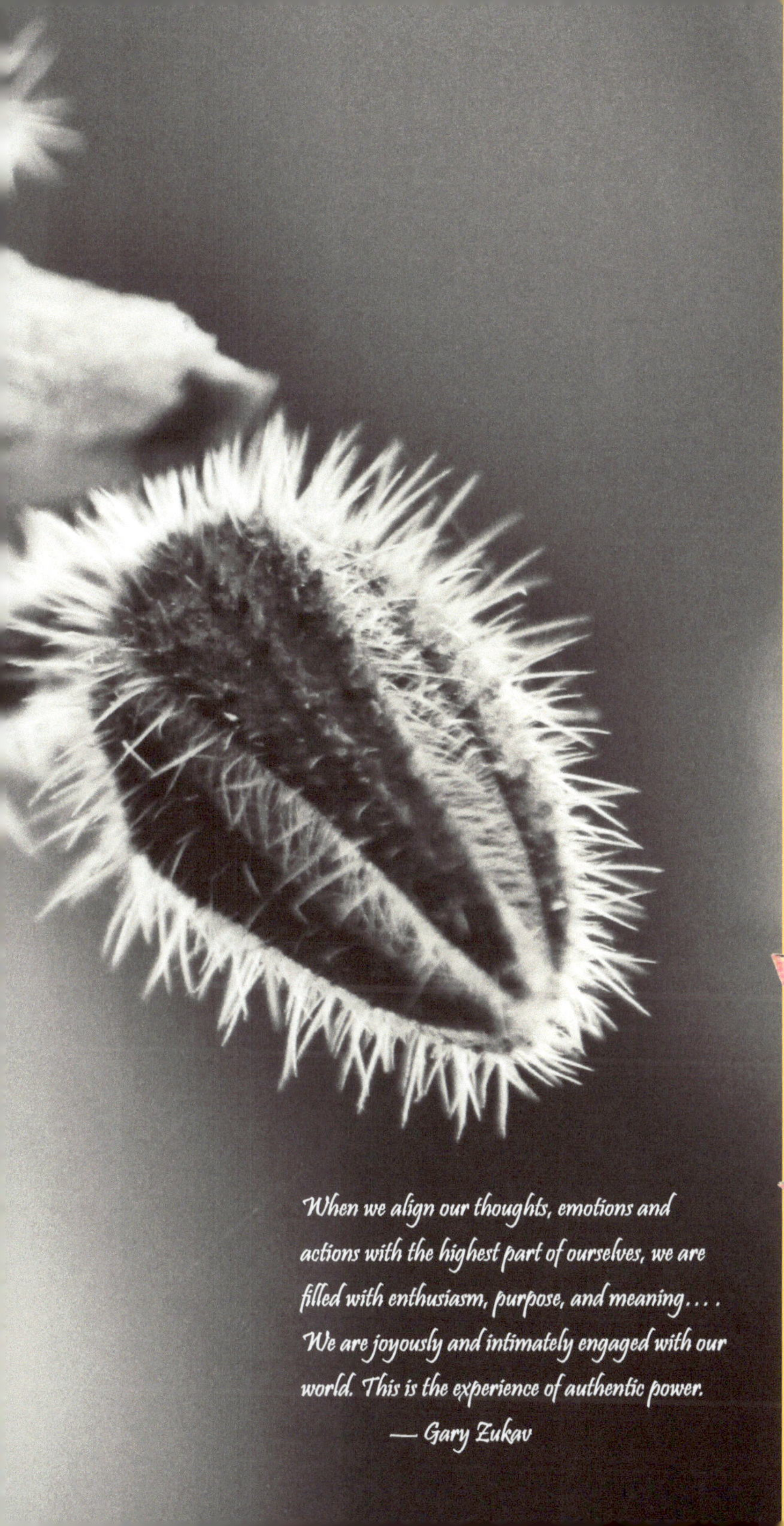

Zone-out from the norm and the "expected ways of thinking and being" you see all around you. Do your best at all times and make your own decisions on how to behave and think. Zone-out to zone-in to your own intuition and creativity, as they are there as your road map to guide you. Love is in you and all around.

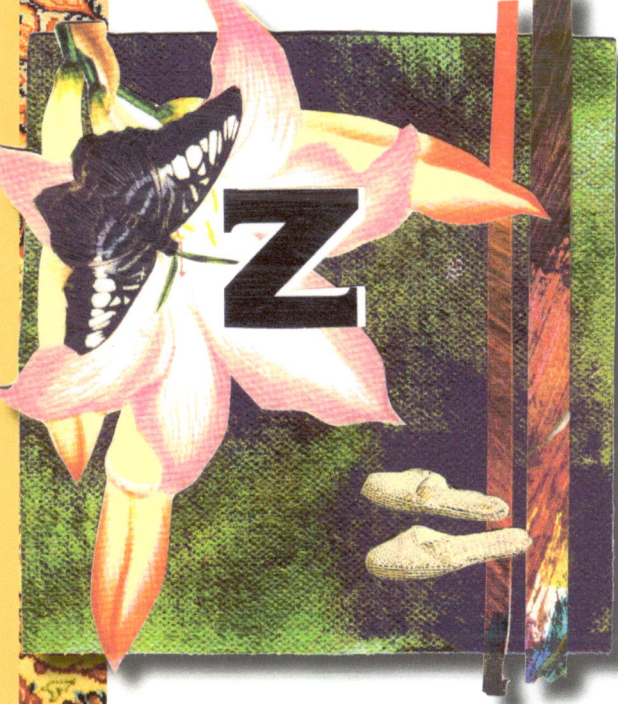

> When we align our thoughts, emotions and actions with the highest part of ourselves, we are filled with enthusiasm, purpose, and meaning.... We are joyously and intimately engaged with our world. This is the experience of authentic power.
> — Gary Zukav

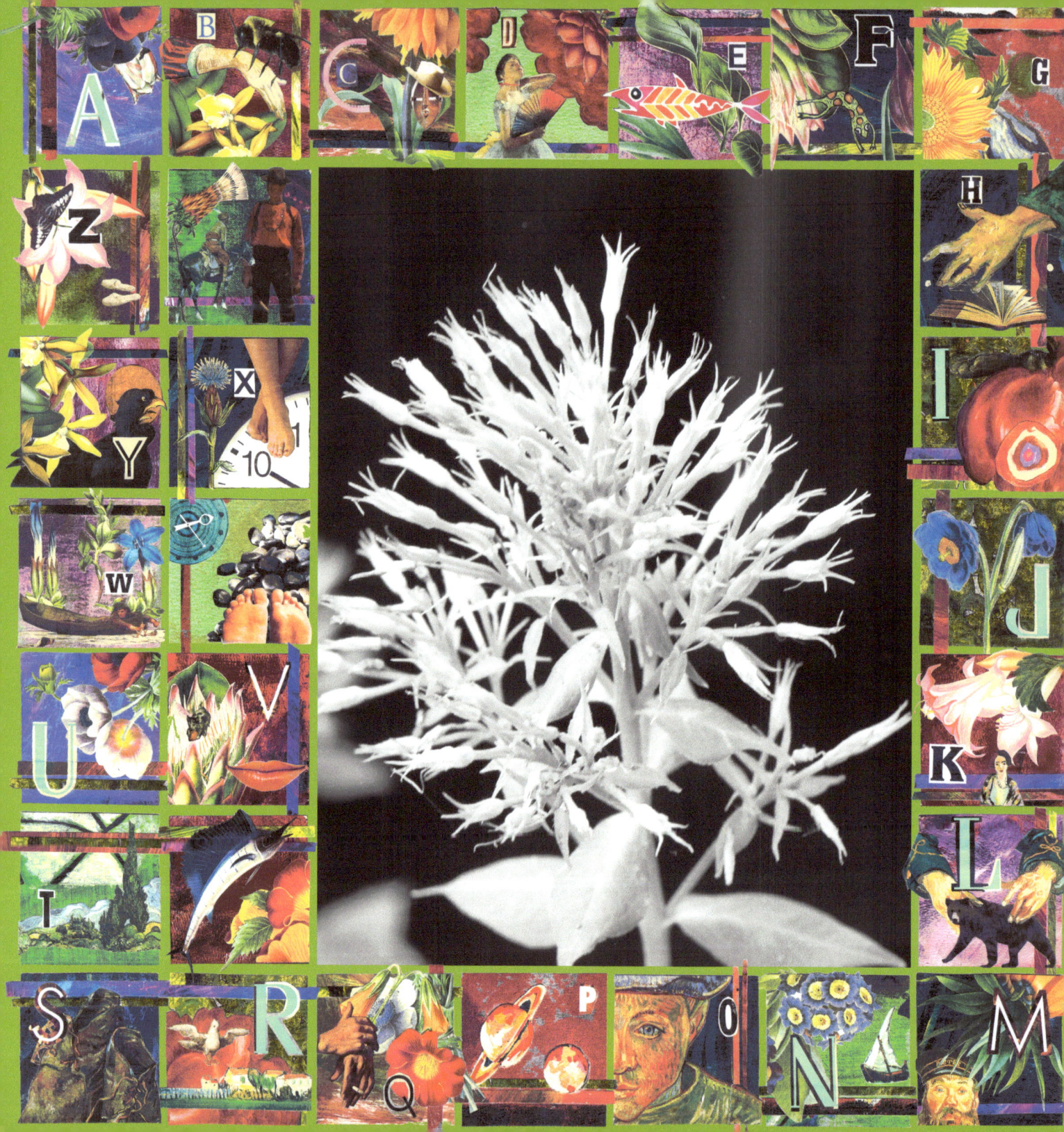